I0457871

CAMBRIDGE

DYNASTY PRESS

Cambridge Dynasty Press
30 N Gould St Ste R
Sheridon, WY 82801
Email: Camdynpress@gmail.com

Cover design by Arina Avakian
Illustrations by Jian Lee

Printed in the United States of America

978-1-955650-09-0 (Paperback)
978-1-955650-06-9 (E-book)
978-1-955650-04-5 (Hardback)

Publisher's Cataloging-in-Publication Data

Park, Jungho, 2025
        How to speak K-drama : cracking the K-drama code and understanding the social cues, life rituals, and hidden meanings beyond subtitles / by Jungho Park.
Series: How to Speak K ; Book 2 | Includes illustrations and a pronunciation appendix.
LCCN 2025916415
LCSH: Korean language--Textbooks for foreign speakers--English. | Korean language--Spoken Korean. | Korean drama--History and criticism. | Popular culture--Korea (South). | Korea (South)--Social life and customs.
LCC PL913 .P37 2025 | DDC 495.782421--dc23

47678459

How to Speak
K-DRAMA

Cracking the K-Drama Code and
Understanding the Social Cues, Life Rituals,
and Hidden Meanings beyond Subtitles

Jungho Park

The greatest drama isn't on the screen.
It's in the journey between two souls from
two different worlds, trying to find one shared
language.

-Jungho Park

The fateful first encounter from *Crash Landing on You*

How to Speak K-DRAMA

Table of Contents

Part 3: The Life Code
Decoding How They Live

Introduction

Have you ever been watching a K-drama, completely lost in the story, but a tiny part of your brain whispers, *"Wait... I feel like I'm missing something?"*

You're not wrong. You *are* missing something.

Subtitles can translate the words, but they can't translate the culture. They tell you *what* a character said, but they can't explain the deep cultural reason *why* they said it that way.

That's why this book is different. We believe there's a huge difference between just watching K-dramas and being able to truly speak K-drama. To "speak" doesn't mean reciting lines from memory. It means fluently understanding the culture *behind* the lines— the unspoken rules, the hidden meanings, and the entire social 'operating system' that makes K-dramas so uniquely addictive.

This book is about turning those "Wait, what just happened?" moments into "Aha! Now I get it!" moments.

It is your cultural playbook for that world. In the following chapters, we'll crack the Verbal, Social, and Life Codes together, using witty analysis, practical 'Playbooks,' and 'Level-Up Vocabulary' from the dramas you love.

By the end of this book, the next time you watch your favorite show, that little voice in your head won't be whispering, "I think I'm missing something." It will be shouting, "Aha! Now I get it."

Ready to go beyond the subtitles? Let's get to work.

A Note from the Author

 When I was a middle school student growing up in the harbor city of Busan, South Korea, my world revolved around two American TV shows: *The X-Files* and *Friends*.

Back then, there was no Netflix, no instant subtitles. I'd wait impatiently, sometimes for weeks, for a fan to upload a Korean subtitle file. More often than not, I'd get the English script and try to translate it myself with a dictionary. But I always hit a wall. I could understand the words, but I couldn't understand the *world*. I could translate Ross's line, but I had no idea *why* the audience was laughing. The culture felt like an invisible barrier that subtitles alone could never break down. I had no one to ask for an explanation.

Years later, after living in the U.S. for a long time and truly understanding the culture, I re-watched those same episodes. Suddenly, it all clicked. The jokes were hilarious. The references made sense. It was an exhilarating "Aha!" moment.

That's when I thought: *This must be what it feels like for K-drama fans.*

I realized that to truly learn a language, you have to understand the culture, the hidden meanings, and the people first. Then, the language comes naturally. That's why I started writing these books—to help tear down that cultural wall for fellow fans like you.

Of course, not everything you see in a K-drama is realistic (I promise you, not all CEOs look like K-pop idols). But what K-dramas do, better than almost anything else, is capture a bittersweet portrait of modern Korea. It's a portrait that contains all of our real-life hopes and anxieties, the latest trends and deep-seated traditions, and our relentless desire to find a little bit of magic in an ordinary day. And I believe that's *why* these stories resonate so deeply with people all over the world. Because when you look past the language barrier, you're seeing a human story of love, struggle, and the incredible resilience of the human heart. If you've ever felt that unexplainable pull, that feeling of "I don't know why, but I *get* this"...

you were feeling just that.

And trust me, I am a fan. I know the feeling of a K-drama finale leaving you with that 'can't-breathe-without-the-next-episode' feeling. I know the strategic pain of saving a new series for weeks, because you know the second you start Episode 1, you won't be able to stop until you see the end.

That passion, combined with my experience as a language educator, led to my first book, How to Speak KPOP, which became a Hottest New Release and Bestseller on Amazon.

Now, with this book, I want to give you that same "Aha!" moment I felt. This isn't a textbook. This is your personal decoder for the world beyond the subtitles. By the end, you won't just *watch* K-dramas; you'll be able to truly speak them.

That "Aha!" moment of finally understanding is an amazing feeling, and I hope this book brings you many of them.

P.S. I love hearing from fellow fans and readers. You can always reach me at: theauthorjp@gmail.com

How to Use This Book

So, you've decided to go beyond the subtitles. Great!

You're holding more than just a book; you're holding a master key to the world beyond them. Because this book is a little different from your typical Korean textbook, here's a quick guide on how to get the most out of our adventure together.

The best way to explain our format is to simply show you. Think of this as a special **"Chapter 0."**

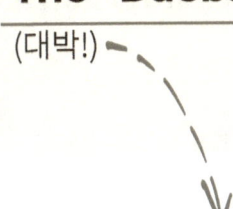

The "Daebak!" Moment

(대박!)

That's **Hangul**, the awesome Korean alphabet!

You'll see it in parentheses like this throughout the book. **Don't panic!** We've included it for curious readers, but you absolutely **do not** need to learn Hangul to understand the codes in this book. We'll give you everything you need with our easy-to-read romanizations - which is just a fancy term for spelling out Korean sounds using English letters.

So relax. Your only assignment is to have fun.

EXAMPLE

 **A Quick Pronunciation Tip for This Chapter**

Let's start with a fun one: 대박 (**dae-bak**).

☑ 대 (**dae**): Say the English word "**day**" out loud. It sounds like "deh-ee," right? Just drop the "ee" sound at the end. It's the clean, sharp "**deh**" sound without the 'y' trail.

☑ 박 (**bak**): Sounds like the "**bark**" of a dog, but stop the sound before you get to the 'r'. It's a short, clipped "**bak**."

You see it all the time. A character discovers a shocking secret or witnesses something amazing, and their eyes go wide as they exclaim, "대박! (**Daebak!**)" This single word is the ultimate Korean exclamation for anything awesome, shocking, or unbelievable.

EXAMPLE

The **DECODER'S** Playbook

Here's a pro-tip based on questions often seen on online fan forums or real-life struggles that foreigners experience in South Korea, giving you the cheat codes to handle these situations like a pro.

The Pro-Tip: Is Daebak always positive? Not necessarily! A bright, excited "Daebak!" is a genuine amazement. A low, sighing "Daebak..." is pure sarcasm.

⬆ Level-Up Vocabulary

대박나다 (**Daebak-nada, dae-bak-na-da**) To have a huge success; to hit the jackpot. This is the verb form. You'll often hear characters wishing their friends' new business "대박 나세요! (Daebak-naseyo!)"—"I hope it becomes a huge hit!"

EXAMPLE

Our Final Pro-Tip: There Are No Rules! This isn't a textbook you have to read from front to back. Feel free to jump around! If a chapter title about soju etiquette or the 'Spoon Class System' catches your eye, dive right in. Every chapter is its own satisfying discovery.

The first code is waiting. Turn the page.

PART 1:

The Verbal Code
(대사 속에 숨겨진 진짜 뜻)

Let's be real: subtitles are liars.

Not in a malicious way, of course. They try their best, but they're just not telling you the whole story. Think of K-drama dialogue as a giant iceberg. The subtitles are the small, visible tip you see floating above the water. They give you the basic plot points, sure. But the real drama—the secret confessions, the subtle power plays, the inside jokes—is all hidden in the massive 90% that lies beneath the surface.

This part of the book is your scuba gear.

We're about to dive deep into the verbal codes that native speakers understand instinctively. We'll decode the titles that define a relationship, the casual phrases that are actually packed with meaning, and the different ways to say "sorry" that can either save a friendship or start a war.

By the end of this part, you won't just be *watching* the conversation. You'll be *in* on it.

Ready to see what the subtitles have been hiding?

The beautiful and poetic world of *Goblin*

 **A Quick Pronunciation Tip for Chapter 1**

Hey! To really feel the drama in this chapter, let's get a handle on a few key sounds.

☑ 애 (ae): Sounds like the 'a' in "**a**pple" or "**a**dd." A bright, open sound. You'll find it in 대 (dae).

☑ 어 (eo): It's a chill and relaxed vowel. Like the 'u' in "**su**n." You'll find it in 선 (seon).

☑ 오 (o): Make a perfect 'O' with your lips, like the 'o' in "sn**ow**."

☑ ㅃ (pp): This is a "tense" sound with no puff of air. Try this: 1. Press your lips together firmly. 2. Without letting any air escape first, make a short, sharp "ppa!" sound. It's a quick, tight sound.

Got it? Awesome. Now you're ready to play the game.

The Ultimate Title Guide

(오빠, 선배, 대표님?)

You know the scene. The female lead is standing a few feet away from her impossibly handsome, notoriously aloof boss. The air is thick with unspoken tension. In her head, a civil war is raging. Should she stick with the safe, formal **대표님 (dae-pyo-nim)**? Or should she take the leap... and call him something else?

Welcome to the most high-stakes game in K-drama: The Korean Title Game. This isn't just about being polite. This is verbal chess, where a single word can define your past, present, and—most importantly—your romantic future. Honestly, it's the K-drama equivalent of updating your relationship status on Facebook or going Instagram official for everyone to see.

Let's decode the three key titles that map out this epic journey.

First up, the starting block: **대표님 (dae-pyo-nim)**. This title, meaning "CEO" or "Representative Director," is The Formal Wall. It's the sound of pure, unadulterated business. It's respectful, safe, and builds a professional barrier so high you'd need a construction permit to get over it. In **[스타트업, Start-Up; 2020, Netflix],** the entire plot revolves around the characters growing into the weight and responsibility of the title **Daepyonim (대표님)**. It's the definitive signifier of a professional relationship, full of potential but locked behind a formal title.

But then, things start to get interesting. A character makes a clever move. They switch to 선배 **(seon-bae)**. This word for "senior" (in a field or from school) is a total game-changer. It artfully dissolves the corporate hierarchy and swaps it out with a social one, one built on shared experience. It says, "I see you as more than just my boss. We share a connection." The wall isn't gone, but a door has just creaked open. It's the beginning of a beautiful... complication.

Finally, we have the main event, the one word that sends fans screaming at their screens: 오빠 **(o-ppa)**. While it literally means "older brother" for a female speaker, using it in a romantic context is the nuclear option. It obliterates the last remnants of formality and pulls a person into the speaker's most intimate circle.

In [김비서가 왜 그럴까, **What's Wrong with Secretary Kim; 2018, Hulu/Viki**], the tension of switching from a formal title (in this case, the even more powerful vice president, which functions just like **Daepyonim** (대표님)) to **Oppa** (오빠) drives the entire romance. This is also the central conflict in [사내맞선, **Business Proposal; 2022, Netflix**]. The moment that formal title disappears for good, the "fake" relationship becomes 100% real.

But understanding the meaning of these titles is just the first step. To truly master the game in real life, you need to know the plays. Let's add the key strategies to your playbook.

The DECODER'S Playbook

Here are the three essential plays for navigating Korean social titles in the real world.

Play #1: The "When in Doubt, Go Formal" Play

The Pro-Tip: Not sure what to call someone? Always, always default to the most respectful title and formal language (**Jondaetmal**). You will never offend someone by being too polite, but you can definitely cause majorly awkward drama by being too casual. This is your safest opening move.

Play #2: The "Title Over Age" Play (in the office)

The Pro-Tip: Your boss is younger than you? It feels weird, but the rule is clear: title trumps age. Address them respectfully as Daepyonim (대표님). Trying to act like the "older, wiser one" is a rookie mistake. Respect the position, and you'll earn their respect in return.

Play #3: The "High-Risk, High-Reward" Oppa Play

The Pro-Tip: Thinking of calling a male colleague or acquaintance Oppa? Use extreme caution. This play should only be run when you are 100% sure you are in a mutual Sseom or already close friends. Using it too early can be seen as overly familiar or even flirtatious. Using it at the right time, however, can be the perfect move to level up your relationship.

Level-Up Vocabulary

...님 (Nim, nim) The Instant Respect Suffix. This is the magic particle you attach to a name or title to instantly make it formal and respectful. 대표 (daepyo) is a CEO; 대표님 (daepyo-nim) is *your* CEO, whom you respect. Think of it as a built-in "Sir/Ma'am."

후배 (Hoobae, hu-bae) A junior colleague or student. This is the other half of the 선배 (seonbae) relationship. A hoobae is expected to show respect, and in return, the sunbae is expected to buy them food and offer sage life advice. This symbiotic relationship is the engine that runs every K-drama workplace.

누나 (Nuna, nu-na) What a male calls an older sister or a slightly older female friend/romantic interest. This is the magic word that officially kicks off any "Noona Romance." When the younger male lead finally drops a formal title and calls her nuna, he no longer sees her as just a friend or a colleague—he sees her as a woman.

형 **(Hyeong, hyeong)** What a male calls an older brother or a slightly older male friend. This is the foundation of every great K-drama "bromance." It signifies loyalty, brotherhood, and a deep, non-romantic bond between men. When a character calls someone hyeong, he's saying, "I trust you, and I've got your back."

언니 **(Eonni, un-nee)** What a female calls an older sister or a slightly older female friend. The cornerstone of female solidarity, or "sismance." Whether they're ganging up on a terrible ex-boyfriend or sharing late-night snacks, the eonni-dongsaeng (younger sibling) relationship is a powerful force.

나이 **(Nai, nah-ee)** Age. Why are Koreans so "obsessed" with age? This is why. Asking someone's nai isn't rude; it's essential for social data-gathering. It allows you to immediately calculate who is the eonni, oppa, or dongsaeng, which determines which "language mode" (formal or casual) to use. It's the first step in mapping out any new relationship. A bit confusing at first, but you're getting the hang of it, right?

 **The Two Keywords for Chapter 2**

Before you start this quest, let's make sure you have the right "magic words." The key to this chapter is distinguishing between these two terms:

☑ 존댓말 (**jon-daen-mal**): This is the formal, polite speech we've been talking about.

☑ 반말 (**ban-mal**): This is the casual, informal speech you're about to unlock. To pronounce 반 (**ban**) correctly, think of the vowel sound in "sp**a**" or "f**a**ther." It's that open "ah" sound. Just put a 'b' in front and an 'n' at the end. Try saying "**bahn**."

That's it! You're ready to start the quest!

Level Up: The Banmal Quest

(관계 레벨업: 반말 퀘스트)

Welcome to the first major "quest" in any K-drama relationship, a mission far more nerve-wracking than defusing a bomb or exposing a corrupt CEO. We're talking about the quest to switch from the polite, formal **존댓말 (jon-daen-mal)** to the casual, informal **반말 (ban-mal)**.

Think of it this way: Jondaetmal is the default language setting for the entire K-drama universe. It's the language of respect, politeness, and most importantly, *distance*. It's how you talk to your boss, your friend's parents, or that handsome stranger you just met. It builds a safe, respectful, but invisible wall between people.

Banmal, on the other hand, is the language of the inner circle. It's the language of true friends, siblings, and, yes, lovers. It's the ultimate sign that the wall has come down. It's the linguistic equivalent of being given a key to their apartment—you now have access to their most comfortable, unguarded self.

But here's the catch: you can't just decide to start using `Banmal`. That would be like trying to skip to the final boss level in a video game—it's rude and you're not ready for it. You have to earn it. You have to complete the Banmal Quest.

There are two main ways to clear this quest:

1. **The Official Invitation:** The older or more senior person explicitly gives permission. They'll say something like, "우리 말 놓을까? (`Woo-ri mal no-eul-kka?`)" which means, "Should we drop the formalities?" This is the official green light.

2. **The Unspoken Agreement:** During a moment of high emotion—a dangerous situation, a heartfelt confession—one person starts using `Banmal` out of instinct, and the other person accepts it without question. The rules are broken, and a new relationship is forged in the chaos.

The perfect example of **The Official Invitation** comes from **[응답하라 1988, Reply 1988; 2015, Netflix/Viki]**. Sun-woo is secretly dating the older, fiery Bo-ra. He desperately wants to drop the formalities, but she's the older one, so he can't. The moment she finally looks at him and says, "야, 김선우. 너 나한테 반말 쓰지 마." (Hey, Kim Sun-woo. Don't you use Banmal with me.), only to follow it up with a shy "...라고 할 줄 알았지?" (...is what you thought I'd say?), she gives him the official permission. It's a huge, heart-fluttering level-up moment for their relationship.

For **The Unspoken Agreement**, look no further than [사랑의 불시착, **Crash Landing on You; 2019, Netflix**]. Captain Ri Jeong-hyeok, a North Korean soldier, almost always speaks formal Jondaetmal to the South Korean heiress Yoon Se-ri, maintaining a respectful distance. But in moments of extreme danger, when he's protecting her, he instinctively switches to Banmal. His words become more direct, more commanding, and paradoxically, more intimate. He doesn't ask for permission; the urgency of the situation grants it for him, and in doing so, reveals his true feelings.

Another great example is the military romance [태양의 후예, **Descendants of the Sun; 2016, Viki/ Netflix**]. The two leads, a soldier and a doctor, start their relationship with the strictly formal language required by their high-stakes jobs. But as they face life-and-death situations together, the Jondaetmal barrier begins to crack, and they start mixing in Banmal, signaling that their connection is becoming personal and profound.

And it's in these pivotal moments that the director uses another powerful code: the Original Soundtrack, or OST. The swell of Gummy's iconic ballad, "You Are My Everything," doesn't just add to the mood; it *confirms* the relationship level-up for the audience. The music becomes the official announcement that their Sseom is over, often before the characters even say it out loud.

So, next time you watch a drama, keep your ears open. When the language shifts, you'll know the characters haven't just changed their words—they've leveled up their entire relationship.

But how do you complete this high-stakes quest in the real world without accidentally offending someone? It's tricky, but not impossible. Here are the essential plays for your Banmal Quest.

The **DECODER'S Playbook**

You've learned the difference between the formal Jondaetmal and the casual Banmal. Here are the three most important plays to remember when navigating this in real life.

Play #1: The "Wait for the Green Light" Play

The Pro-Tip: This is the golden rule. If you are the younger or more junior person, you *never* initiate the switch to Banmal yourself. It's the older/more senior person's role to grant permission. You must wait for them to give you the green light, often by saying, "**우리 말 놓자 (Woo-ri mal no-cha)**" or "**말 편하게 해 (Mal pyeon-hage hae)**"—"Let's speak comfortably." This is your official invitation to level up.

Play #2: The "Same-Age Shortcut" Play

The Pro-Tip: Find out you're the same age (**동갑, dong-gap**) as a new Korean acquaintance? Congratulations, you've found a social shortcut! In Korea, people born in the same year can often become **친구 (chingu)** and switch to Banmal very quickly. It's perfectly acceptable to ask, "**혹시 우리… 동갑인데 말 놓을까? (Hoksi uri... dong-gab-inde mal no-eul-kka?)**"—"Hey, since we're the same age… should we drop the formalities?"

Play #3: The "Emotional Wall" Play

The Pro-Tip: The switch isn't always permanent. In K-dramas, watch what happens after a major fight between a couple or close friends. A character who was using Banmal might suddenly switch *back* to the formal Jondaetmal. This is a devastatingly effective power move. It's a way of building an instant emotional wall and saying, "Right now, we are not close." It's the ultimate passive-aggressive signal that you're in the danger zone.

⬆ Level-Up Vocabulary

말을 놓다 (`Mareul nota, ma-reul no-ta`) Literally "to let go of speech," this is the essential idiomatic phrase for "to drop formalities" and start speaking Banmal. This is an action that is almost always initiated by the older person as a sign of permission. Hearing "우리 말 놓을까요? (`Woo-ri mal no-eul-kka-yo?`)" is like being handed a key to a new level of friendship.

말을 높이다 (`Mareul nopida, ma-reul no-pi-da`) The opposite of the above, this literally means "to heighten speech." This is what happens when a relationship turns sour or formal again. After a big fight, a couple who used Banmal might suddenly switch back to formal Jondaetmal. It's a devastatingly effective way to build an instant emotional wall and a classic K-drama trope for showing conflict.

동갑 (`Dong-gap, dong-gap`) A person who is the same age as you. In Korea, finding out you're dong-gap with someone is a magic moment. It dissolves the complicated age hierarchy, and you can often become 친구 (`chingu`) and switch to Banmal almost immediately. It's a social shortcut to friendship.

친구 **(Chingu, chin-gu)** Friend. While this seems simple, in Korea, you typically only become true chingu with people of the same age (동갑). This is why characters often ask each other's birth year. It's not just small talk; it's a way to see if they can officially become friends and drop the Jondaetmal.

어색하다 **(Eosaekhada, uh-saek-a-da)** To be awkward. This is the primary emotion felt during the transition from Jondaetmal to Banmal. The first time a character tries to call their older boss Oppa or a new friend by their first name casually, the scene is almost always filled with a charming, cringey, and very relatable awkwardness.

 **A Quick Pronunciation Tip for Chapter 3**

Before we dive into the art of apologizing, let's master this chapter's key sounds.

☑ 죄 **(joe):** This one looks tricky, but it's easy! The ㅚ vowel sounds just like the '**we**' in "**we**dding" or "**wet**." So, just say "jwe."

☑ 송 **(song):** Sounds exactly like the English word "song."

☑ 미 **(mi):** Sounds just like the English word "**me**."

☑ 안 **(an):** Say **"Ah"** (like you would at the doctor's office) and simply add an **"n"** sound to the end. It's the first syllable in the Korean word for "hello," **An-**nyeong (안-녕).

Now you're ready to say sorry like a pro.

The Two Faces of "Sorry"

(미안해 vs. 죄송합니다)

Let's talk about apologies. In your world, there's a universe of difference between a formally written "I sincerely apologize for my actions" and a quick text to your friend that just says "srry." One is for saving your career; the other is for saving your friendship.

In Korean, this difference isn't just about tone—it's built right into the language with two completely distinct words: the heavy, serious 죄송합니다 (joe-song-ham-ni-da) and the much lighter, personal 미안해 (mi-an-hae).

Think of these two words as opposite ends of the "Apology Spectrum."

On one end, you have 죄송합니다 (joesonghamnida). This is your formal, public, bow-at-the-waist apology. This is the word you use when you've spilled coffee on your CEO, insulted your significant other's grandmother, or accidentally started a huge incident. It acknowledges a power imbalance or a serious mistake. It says, "I recognize my fault within our social structure and formally request your forgiveness." In [이태원 클라쓰, **Itaewon Class; 2020, Netflix**], the entire story is built on the main character, Park Sae-ro-yi, refusing to say this single phrase to a powerful CEO. For him, saying Joesonghamnida (죄송합니다) isn't just an apology; it's an act of submission. That's how much weight this word carries.

On the other end of the spectrum, you have 미안해 (**mianhae**). This is your "srry" text. It's the "my bad" you say to a friend when you're five minutes late, or the "oops, sorry" when you bump into them. It's used between people who are close—friends, siblings, partners. The goal isn't to beg for formal forgiveness but to smooth things over and maintain a good relationship. In [응답하라 **1988, Reply 1988; 2015, Netflix/Viki**], the friends constantly get into small arguments and reconcile with a mumbled, slightly awkward Mian (미안)... or Mianhada (미안하다). It's the sound of intimacy and the small, everyday work of maintaining a friendship.

The true drama often lies in the absence of these words. In [더 글로리, **The Glory; 2022, Netflix**], the entire revenge plot is fueled by the fact that the bullies never offered a single, sincere apology—neither a formal Joesonghamnida (죄송합니다) for their crimes nor a personal Mianhae (미안해) for the pain they caused.

So, the next time a character apologizes, listen closely. Are they sending a formal letter, or are they sending a quick text? The word they choose tells you everything you need to know about the gravity of the situation and the nature of their relationship.

But what about when you have to be the one to apologize in Korea? Choosing the right "sorry" is a critical social skill. Let's add the essential plays to your survival kit.

The **DECODER'S** Playbook

You've learned the difference between the heavy `Joesonghamnida` and the casual `Mianhae`. Here are the three most important plays for apologizing like a pro in real life.

Play #1: The "Assess the Damage" Play

The Pro-Tip: Before you apologize, quickly assess the situation. Did you make a simple mistake (실수, `silsu`) or a real fault (잘못, `jalmot`)? Did you offend a close friend or a respected elder? A simple rule of thumb: if you bump into a friend and make them spill their coffee, a heartfelt 미안해 (`mianhae`) is perfect. If you spill that same coffee on your new boss's laptop, you start with a deep bow and an immediate 죄송합니다 (`joesonghamnida`).

Play #2: The "When in Doubt, Go Formal" Play

The Pro-Tip: Are you stuck and not sure which apology to use? Your safest move is to go with the more formal option: 죄송합니다 (`joesonghamnida`). Using a formal apology in a casual situation might be slightly awkward, but they'll just think you're very polite. Using a casual apology in a formal situation can be seen as genuinely rude. It's the safest bet.

Play #3: The "Empathetic 'Sorry'" Play

The Pro-Tip: Sometimes, 미안해 (mianhae) isn't about admitting fault. It can be used to say, "I'm sorry that you're hurting." In K-dramas, when a character is crying about a problem you didn't cause, a friend might hug them and say, "울지마, 나도 미안해 (Wooljima, nado mianhae)"—"Don't cry, it makes me feel sorry, too." It's a way of showing deep empathy and sharing their emotional burden.

⬆ Level-Up Vocabulary

사과하다 (Sagwahada, sa-gwa-ha-da) To apologize. This is the formal verb for the act of apologizing. While 미안해 (mianhae) is saying "I'm sorry," 사과해 (sagwahae)! is a demand: "Apologize to me!" In dramas, when a character demands a formal apology (사과), it's a sign that the situation has escalated beyond a simple misunderstanding.

용서하다 (Yongseohada, yong-suh-ha-da) To forgive. This is the other side of the apology coin. Forgiveness (용서, yongseo) is a major theme in K-dramas. Often, a character will say, "저는 절대로 용서 못 해요 (Jeoneun jeoldae-ro yongseo mot haeyo)," meaning "I can never forgive you," which fuels the plot for many episodes to come.

실수 (Silsu, shil-soo) A mistake; an error. This is for an unintentional mess-up, like spilling coffee or sending a text to the wrong person. It implies a lack of intention. A character might say 이건 내 실수야 (ee-geon nae silsu-ya), "This is my mistake," which is a lighter admission than saying it's their "fault."

잘못 (**Jalmot**, `jal-mot`) A fault; a wrongdoing. This is heavier than silsu. It implies that you are to blame and that what you did was wrong, not just an accident. When a character admits, 내 잘못이야 (`nae jalmo-siya`), "It's my fault," it's a true admission of guilt and a much more significant step than admitting a simple mistake.

후회하다 (**Huhoehada**, `hoo-hweh-ha-da`) To regret. The feeling that powers almost every dramatic apology. K-drama protagonists are masters of regret, often staring into the rain while thinking about their past actions. A sincere apology is often followed by a heartfelt confession of how much they regret their 잘못 (`jalmot`).

섭섭하다 (**Seopseop-hada**, `sup-sup-a-da`) To feel sad, disappointed, or let down by someone you're close to. This is a uniquely Korean emotional term. It's not angry, just… disappointed. It's the feeling you get when your best friend forgets your birthday or your partner doesn't take your side. It's the perfect emotion to trigger a heartfelt 미안해 (`mianhae`).

 **A Quick Pronunciation Tip for Chapter 4**

This chapter's keyword looks like a monster, but it's easy when you break it down. Let's look at 괜찮아요 (**gwaen-chan-a-yo**).

☑️ 괜 (**gwaen**) : This is a quick one! It sounds just like the name "**Gwen**" (like Gwen Stacy).

☑️ 찮 (**chan**) : Sounds like the first part of "**Chan**el" or a "**chan**ce."

☑️ 아 (**a**) : Our old friend, the "Ah" sound from the doctor's office.

☑️ 요 (**yo**) : Exactly like you're saying "**Yo**!" to a friend.

Put it all together: **Gwen-chan-ah-yo**. You've got it.

The "Gwaenchanayo?" Multi-Tool

(괜찮아요?)

If Korean words were K-drama characters, 사랑해 (saranghae) would be the romantic lead. But the true main character—the one who shows up in every single episode and plays a dozen different roles? That would be 괜찮아요 (gwaenchanayo). This single phrase is the Swiss Army knife of the Korean language. It can mean "Are you okay?", "I'm okay," "Yes, that's fine," and "No, thank you." Yes, you read that right. It can mean both "yes" and "no."

Confused? You're supposed to be. This is where subtitles often throw their hands up in defeat, because the true meaning isn't in the word itself—it's in the tone, the context, and the subtle flicker in the character's eyes.

Let's unpack this ultimate multi-tool.

1. The Question: "Are you okay?" (괜찮아요?)

- This is the easiest one to spot. When the intonation goes up at the end of the sentence, it's a question. After someone trips, cries, or has the mother of a chaebol (the Korean version of a billionaire heir from a powerful, family-run corporate dynasty) throws water in their face, another character will rush to their side and ask, Gwaenchanayo? This is a pure, simple concern.

2. The Reassurance: "I'm okay." (괜찮아요.)

- This is the standard reply to the question above, but here's the K-drama twist: it's often used when the character is very clearly not okay. The most iconic example of this can be found in the epic fantasy **[도깨비, Goblin; 2016, Viki]**. In the final battle, the hero, Kim Shin (the Goblin), has the magical sword that has been lodged in his chest for 900 years finally being pulled out. He is in immense, world-ending agony, literally turning to dust. But as the heroine, Ji Eun-tak, weeps in terror, he gives her a sad, beautiful smile and reassures her that he's fine, telling her not to worry. His 'I'm okay' in this moment is the ultimate act of love—a desperate attempt to protect the person he loves from the horror of his own pain.

3. The Polite Refusal: "No, thank you." (아니요, 괜찮아요.)

- This is the advanced level, the one that causes the most confusion. When someone offers you something—a drink, a ride home, a promotion—replying with a slightly smiling, head-shaking Gwaenchanayo almost always means "No, thank you." It's a culturally polite way of refusing without being blunt. In [힘쎈여자 도봉순, **Strong Woman Do Bong Soon; 2017, Viki/Netflix**], you'll see countless scenes where characters politely refuse offers of food or help with this phrase, not wanting to impose on others.

4. The Acceptance: "Yes, that's fine." / "It's okay." (네, 괜찮아요.)

- To make things even more fun, Gwaenchanayo can also mean "yes." This usually happens when someone apologizes for a minor mistake. For example, if a friend says, "Sorry I'm five minutes late!" the natural reply is Gwaenchanayo, meaning "It's okay, no problem." In friendship-focused dramas like [응답하라 **1988, Reply 1988; 2015, Netflix/Viki**], this use is everywhere. It's the oil that keeps social relationships running smoothly.

So, the Gwaenchanayo Multi-Tool is all about context. Is it a question? A tough-guy reassurance? A polite "no"? Or a forgiving "yes"? Now that you know what to look for, you'll be able to decode it every time.

Decoding what you see in a drama is one thing. Knowing how to react in the real world is the next level. To truly master this tricky phrase, let's add the essential plays to your social playbook.

The **DECODER'S** Playbook

You've learned the many faces of Gwaenchanayo. Here are the four essential plays to navigate its beautiful ambiguity in the wild.

Play #1: The "Listen to the Music, Not the Words" Play

The Pro-Tip: The number one clue is the intonation. If the end of the word goes up (괜찮아요?↗), it's almost always a genuine question: "Are you okay?" If the tone is flat or goes down (괜찮아요.↘), it's a statement. This is your first and most important decoding tool.

Play #2: The "Polite Refusal First" Play

The Pro-Tip: When someone offers you something (food, a drink, a gift), and you ask if they want some, their first 괜찮아요 often means "No, thank you." This isn't a lie; it's a polite gesture to avoid seeming greedy or burdensome (부담스럽다). If you really want them to have it, the pro move is to offer a second time. If they refuse again, it's a real "no." If they accept, you've successfully navigated a classic Korean social dance.

Play #3: The "Trust the Eyes, Not the Mouth" Play

The Pro-Tip: A K-drama character is crying while staring into the rain, and their friend asks if they're okay. They will *always* say, "괜찮아 (gwaenchan-a)." They are never okay. In these situations, the word is a defense mechanism. The pro-tip is to ignore the word itself and react to the non-verbal cues—the tears, the sad eyes, the slumped shoulders. That's where the real truth is.

Play #4: The "Are You Really Okay?" Play

The Pro-Tip: If you're on the receiving end of a vague 괜찮아요 in real life and are genuinely confused, the kindest and clearest thing to do is ask a gentle follow-up question. Asking, "**정말 괜찮으세요? (Jeongmal gwaenchanaseyo?)**" - "Are you *really* okay?" shows extra care and can help avoid a major misunderstanding (오해, ohae).

⬆ Level-Up Vocabulary

걱정하다 (**Geokjeonghada, guk-jung-ha-da**) To worry. This is the emotion that powers almost every "괜찮아요? (gwaen-chan-a-yo?)" question. When a character sees their friend looking sad, they'll ask, "무슨 일 있어? 걱정돼 (Museun il isseo? Geokjeong-dwae)," which means "What's wrong? I'm worried." The reply "괜찮아 (gwaen-chan-a)" is meant to soothe that worry.

신경쓰다 (**Sin-gyeong-sseu-da, shin-gyung-sseu-da**) Literally "to use nerves," this phrase means to care about, to be bothered by, or to pay attention to something. It's incredibly versatile. After a character apologizes and the other says "괜찮아 (gwaen-chan-a)," they might add, "신경 쓰지 마 (Sin-gyeong sseuji ma)," meaning "Don't worry about it" or "Never mind." It's the ultimate "let's move on" phrase.

거절하다 (**Geojeolhada, guh-jul-ha-da**) To refuse; to reject. This is the formal verb for what "괜찮아요 (gwaen-chan-a-yo)" often does politely. When a character says, "회장님의 제안을 거절하겠습니다 (Hoejangnim-ui jean-eul geojeolhagesseumnida)," meaning "I will refuse the Chairman's offer," it's a very direct, high-stakes moment. Using "괜찮습니다 (gwaen-chan-sseum-ni-da)" is the much softer, less confrontational way to do the same thing.

부담스럽다 (Budamseureopda, boo-dam-sereup-da) To feel burdened, pressured, or uncomfortable (because something is too much). This is the core feeling that explains **why** Koreans often say "괜찮아요 (gwaen-chan-a-yo)" to refuse something. If a rich character offers a poor character an expensive gift, the recipient might feel budamseureopda. Saying "괜찮아요 (gwaen-chan-a-yo)" is a polite way of saying, "That's too much for me, I feel uncomfortable accepting it."

오해 (Ohae, oh-hae) A misunderstanding. This is the dramatic consequence that frequently happens because of the ambiguity of "괜찮아요 (gwaen-chan-a-yo)." One character says "괜찮아 (gwaen-chan-a)" meaning "I'm okay (but still sad)," but the other character misinterprets it as "It's really okay (so let's forget about it)." This ohae then becomes the fuel for the next episode's conflict.

 **A Quick Pronunciation Tip for Chapter 5**

This chapter's keyword is one you've definitely heard. Let's make sure you're saying it right: 화이팅 (`hwa-i-ting`).

☑ 화 (`hwa`): Think of saying "**wha**t" but with a softer 'h' sound.

☑ 이 (`i`): The easy one! Sounds just like the "ee" in "s**ee**."

☑ 팅 (`ting`): Exactly like the English word "**ting**" (as in, a little bell goes "ting!").

Put it all together: **Hwa-ee-ting!** See? You've been saying it perfectly all along.

The "Fighting!" Energy Boost

(화이팅!)

If you've spent any time in K-dramaland, you've probably noticed something strange. Characters will be facing a big exam, a job interview, or a nerve-wracking confession, and their friends will cheer them on by enthusiastically shouting... "Fighting!"

Your first thought might have been, "Fighting who? Is there about to be a brawl?"

Let's be real: 화이팅 (hwaiting) is the undisputed king of Konglish (Korean-style English). It's a perfect example of taking an English word, completely stripping it of its original aggressive meaning, and re-birthing it as something uniquely, wonderfully Korean.

So, what does it actually mean? Think of it as the quintessential motivational multi-tool. It's a single-word-smoothie blended from "Good luck!", "You can do it!", "Break a leg!", and "Go get 'em!" all rolled into one. It's a burst of positive energy, a verbal fist pump, a magical spell that means: "I'm rooting for you, and I believe in you."

You'll see this magic spell cast in a few key situations:

1. **The Good Luck Charm:** Before a big test or performance. In **[닥터슬럼프, Doctor Slump; 2024, Netflix],** where the main characters are overcoming career burnout, a heartfelt Hwaiting! is a crucial dose of support.

2. **The Roar of the Crowd:** At any sporting event. In the beloved cult classic **[역도요정 김복주, Weightlifting Fairy Kim Bok-joo; 2016, Viki/ Netflix],** the air is thick with cries of Hwaiting! as friends and teammates cheer on the athletes. It's the sound of pure and unadulterated support.

And perhaps the most common use? Cheering for yourself. You'll often see a character, alone in their room before a big day, look in the mirror, pump their own fist, and whisper to their reflection, "Hwaiting." It's a moment of self-reassurance, a personal pep-talk. This is perfectly captured in the classic office drama

[미생, Misaeng: Incomplete Life; 2014, Netflix]. The protagonist, Jang Geu-rae, is a young intern with no college degree, thrown into the brutal corporate world. He often escapes to the company rooftop to catch his breath. In these quiet, lonely moments, you see him looking out at the city, taking a deep breath to steady his nerves, and whispering to himself, "Hwaiting." It's not a loud cheer; it's his personal mantra for survival, the quiet armor he puts on before heading back into the battlefield of the office.

So think of Hwaiting as more than just a word; it's a piece of beautifully efficient cultural technology, a linguistic life hack for generating morale on demand.

And the best part? You can use this life hack right now. Seriously, go on. Thinking about that monstrous pile of laundry, that deadline breathing down your neck, or just the general chaos of being a person? Take a moment, make a small fist for dramatic effect (highly recommended), and say it out loud with a little bit of conviction.

Hwaiting! (화이팅!)

Feel that? That tiny jolt of can-do energy, that subtle shift in your mindset? That's the code running. It's the magic of a word that doesn't just wish you good luck—it helps you create it. You haven't just learned a phrase; you've found the K-drama cheat code for motivating yourself. And every time you shout 'Hwaiting,' you'll discover yourself becoming the protagonist of a K-drama.

And every protagonist needs a powerful magic spell. Hwaiting is now yours to use, but to wield it effectively, you need the right plays. Let's add them to the playbook.

The **DECODER'S** Playbook

You've learned the meaning behind Korea's favorite cheer. Here are the three essential plays to use Hwaiting like a true K-drama fan.

Play #1: The "Future-Facing" Play

The Pro-Tip: The most important rule is that Hwaiting is almost always used for a *future* challenge. It's for wishing luck *before* something happens.

- **Use it for:** an upcoming exam, a job interview, a sports match, a big presentation.
- **Don't use it for:** comforting someone after they've failed or when they are sad. In that situation, the better phrase is the gentler "힘내 (himnae)"—"Stay strong."

Play #2: The "Action Combo" Play

The Pro-Tip: Hwaiting isn't just a word; it's a physical performance. To give it maximum power, you need to add a gesture. The classic move is the small, determined fist pump (주먹 불끈, jumeok bulkkeun). Raise a fist to about chest level, give it a firm but gentle shake, and say "Hwaiting!" with an encouraging smile. It's a combo move of verbal and physical support.

Play #3: The "Mirror Motivation" Play

The Pro-Tip: One of the most powerful ways to use Hwaiting is on yourself. This isn't just a K-drama trope; it's a real-life self-motivation hack. Feeling overwhelmed or nervous? Find a quiet moment (looking in the mirror is optional, but adds excellent dramatic effect), take a deep breath, and whisper or shout "Hwaiting!" to your own reflection. It might feel cheesy for a second, but you'll be surprised by the jolt of can-do energy it provides.

⬆ Level-Up Vocabulary

응원하다 (Eungwonhada, eung-won-ha-da) To cheer for; to support. This is the official verb for the act of cheering someone on. While 화이팅 (hwaiting)! is the chant, 응원 (eungwon) is the concept. A character might say, "제가 항상 응원할게요 (**Jega hangsang eungwonhalgeyo**)" which means, "I'll always be supporting you." It's a promise of loyal support.

기운 (Gi-un, gi-oon) Energy; vigor; spirit. This is a person's life force. When a character looks tired or sad, their friend will say, "기운 내 (gi-un nae)!" which literally means "Put out your energy!" It's a common way to say "Cheer up!" or "Get some energy!" It's the perfect phrase to shout right before a heartfelt Hwaiting!.

힘내다 (Himnaeda, him-nae-da) To put forth strength; to cheer up. This is another phrase very similar to "Cheer up!" but with a nuance of strength (힘, him). While 기운 내 (gi-un nae) is for someone who seems listless, "힘내 (himnae)!" is often for someone facing a known, difficult struggle. It's a way of saying, "Be strong" or "Hang in there."

용기 (Yong-gi, yong-gi) Courage. This is often what a "Hwaiting!" cheer is meant to inspire. In a classic romance trope, one character will give another a small gift or a note "to give them courage" before a big event. This gift is a physical manifestation of the yong-gi they are trying to transfer.

포기하다 (Pogihada, po-gi-ha-da) To give up. This is the ultimate antagonist to the spirit of Hwaiting. The most dramatic K-drama moments often feature a character on the brink of giving up (포기하다), only to be stopped by a friend or loved one who tells them, "포기하지 마 (pogihaji ma)!" — "Don't give up!" This phrase is almost always followed by a powerful, episode-ending Hwaiting!

고생 **(Gosaeng, go-saeng)** Hardship, suffering, and incredible effort that requires a Hwaiting! in the first place. But more importantly, it has a magical phrase associated with it for after the struggle is over. If Hwaiting! is the cheer you shout at the starting line, then **고생했어 (gosaeng-haess-eo)** is the warm hug you give at the finish line. It's what you say to a friend after a brutal exam or a colleague after a stressful project. It means "You've worked so hard," "You've been through a lot," and "I see your struggle." In a culture that values resilience, this is one of the most comforting phrases you can hear.

PART 2:

The Social Code
(관계 속에 숨겨진 약속)

Alright, you've successfully decoded the verbal iceberg of K-dramas. You know what the words *really* mean. But now, welcome to the next level, where the most important rules aren't spoken at all.

This is the social code.

It's the invisible software running in the background of every interaction. It's the silent understanding of why you pour drinks for others but never for yourself, why "our mom" is more natural than "my mom," and how two people can know they're *almost* in a relationship without ever saying a word. This is the world of Jeong (정), Nunchi (눈치), and Sseom (썸)—concepts so deep and nuanced they don't have a simple English translation.

Think of this part of the book as your VIP backstage pass. You're about to learn the secret choreography of Korean relationships—the unspoken rules, the emotional cues, and the social contracts that everyone seems to know without being taught.

Ready to start reading what isn't written?

The heartwarming community crew of *Reply 1988*

 **A Quick Pronunciation Tip for Chapter 6**

This chapter's keyword is 우리 **(u-ri)**. The key here is the letter **'u'**.

Here are two simple rules to remember:

☑ **Rule #1:** In the official Korean romanization, **'u' ALWAYS makes an "oo" sound**, like in "m**oo**n" or "z**oo**." It **never** sounds like the 'u' in "c**u**t."

☑ **Rule #2:** The Korean **'u' is NEVER pronounced like the English word "you."** A perfect example is the word "menu." In English, we say "menyou." But when this word came into Korean, it became 메뉴 **(me-nyu)**. The sound is different.

So, just remember: u = "oo," not "uh" or "you."

That makes **u**ri simple to say: **"oo-ree"**. Master this "u" trick, and you'll pronounce hundreds of other Korean words perfectly!

CHAPTER
Six

The Magic of "Uri"

(우리의 마법)

You're watching a K-drama. The handsome male lead is on the phone, talking about his wife. But what you hear him say is, "**우리 와이프** (`uri` waipeu)," and the subtitle reads, "Our wife." You do a double-take. Wait... *our* wife? Are they sharing?

Relax. He's not in a polygamous relationship. You've just stumbled upon one of the most fundamental and fascinating codes of Korean culture: the magic of **우리 (`uri`)**.

While `uri` does translate to "we" or "our," its meaning goes far deeper than simple possession. It's about a collective identity and a psychological membership. The best way to understand it? Think of how a die-hard sports fan says, "**We** won the championship!" They didn't personally play on the field, but they are emotionally and psychologically part of the team. They share in the victory and identity.

Korean `uri` is like that, but for almost everything. It's a linguistic habit that puts the group before the individual. Using "my" (내, nae) for things like family or school can sound a bit cold, distant, or overly individualistic. Uri implies warmth, a sense of belonging, and a shared identity.

You'll see it everywhere:

- **우리 집 (uri jip)**: "Our house," which really means "My family's house."

- **우리 엄마 (uri eomma)**: "Our mom," which means "My mom."

- **우리 회사 (uri hoesa)**: "Our company," meaning "The company I belong to."

- **우리나라 (uri nara)**: "Our country," the standard way Koreans refer to Korea.

The absolute masterclass in uri culture is [**응답하라 1988, Reply 1988; 2015, Netflix/Viki**]. Think of the iconic scene where the entire neighborhood crams into Taek's tiny room to watch his international Go match, cheering and agonizing as if their own son were competing. When Taek wins, they don't say "Taek won"; they celebrate as if "**we** won." That feeling—his victory being their victory—is the very essence of uri. Here, uri isn't just a word; it's the entire philosophy of their community.

And this powerful sense of "we" isn't just limited to neighbors who become a chosen family. It's also perfectly captured in the deep bonds between colleagues who have been friends for decades, as seen in the beloved drama [슬기로운 의사생활, **Hospital Playlist; 2020-2021, Netflix]**. When one of them faces a difficult surgery, it instantly becomes "**우리 문제 (uri munje)**," our problem. They gather in each other's offices, sharing food and debating diagnoses as if the patient belongs to all of them. Their weekly band practice isn't just a hobby; it's a sacred ritual that reinforces their uri.

So, when you hear uri, don't think of shared ownership. Think of a shared heart. It's a small word that reveals a massive cultural worldview, one that values the collective "we" right alongside the individual "me."

Grasping this beautiful theory is step one. But to navigate this 'we-centric' culture with confidence, you need to know how the code plays out in real life. Let's add the essential plays to your playbook.

The DECODER'S Playbook

You understand the collectivist spirit of uri. Here are the key plays to navigate this "we-centric" culture with confidence.

Play #1: The "Uri is for a Team, Nae is for a Thing" Play

The Pro-Tip: When do you use 우리 (uri) versus 내 (nae) (my)? A simple rule of thumb: if what you're talking about involves a shared identity or group (like family, school, company, country), uri is almost always the more natural choice. "Our company (우리 회사)" sounds more natural than "My company." However, for personal, unshared possessions (my phone, my bag, my coffee), you would always use 내 (nae). Calling your phone "uri phone" would just be weird.

Play #2: The "Welcome to the Uri" Play

The Pro-Tip: What do you do when a Korean friend refers to their mom as "우리 엄마 (uri eomma)" when talking to you? Don't be confused! This is a huge compliment. By using uri instead of nae, they are subconsciously including you in their inner circle for that moment. They are sharing their family's story *with* you. The best response is to just accept it warmly and continue the conversation. It's a subtle invitation into their world.

Play #3: The "National Uri" Play

The Pro-Tip: You will often hear Koreans, even when speaking English, say things like, "In our country, the food is..." or "Our country's national team..." when referring to Korea. This isn't overly nationalistic; it's a direct translation of the 우리나라 (uri nara) mindset. It's a linguistic habit that reflects a strong collective national identity. It's a fascinating code to spot in everyday conversation.

Level-Up Vocabulary

정 (**Jeong, jung**) A deep, emotional connection and affection that binds people together. Jeong is the invisible glue of every 우리 (uri) community. It's more than love, more than friendship. It's the warmth you feel for the people in your life, the reason you share your side dishes, and the feeling that makes a friend's joy or sorrow feel like your own. It's one of the most important and beautiful concepts in Korean culture.

식구 (**Sikgu, shik-goo**) Family members; "one family." The literal translation of sikgu is "food mouths," meaning the people you share meals (밥, bap) with. This beautiful word shows how deeply the act of eating together is tied to the concept of family and belonging in Korea. When a K-drama character says, "이제 우리는 한 식구야 (Ije urineun han sikgu-ya)," ("We're one family now"), it's the ultimate declaration of acceptance into their uri.

내 편 (Nae pyeon, nae-pyun) My side; my person; my team. This is a powerful declaration of loyalty. When a character is in trouble and asks, "넌 내 편이지? (Neon nae pyeon-iji?)"—"You're on my side, right?"—they're asking for unconditional support. Having someone who is nae pyeon means having an ally who will defend you no matter what, a core function of a strong uri.

남 (Nam, nahm) An outsider; a stranger; "not one of us." To understand the concept of uri (us), you have to understand its opposite: nam. Nam is anyone outside your circle of family, friends, and colleagues. In K-dramas, you'll often hear characters say, "우리는 남이잖아 (Urineun nam-ijana)," meaning "We're strangers," to draw a clear line and establish emotional distance.

공동체 (Gongdongche, gong-dong-cheh) A community; a collective. This is the larger concept that uri culture is built upon. Whether it's a family, a village, a company team, or a group of friends living in the same neighborhood like in [응답하라 1988, Reply 1988], the sense of **gongdongche** is what makes individual struggles a shared responsibility and individual joys a collective celebration.

 **A Quick Tip & Culture Dive for Chapter 7**

Before we solve the mystery of "Let's grab a meal," we first need to understand the magic of the keyword itself: 밥 (**bap**).

First, the pronunciation: when the ㅂ consonant is at the end, your lips just gently close to stop the sound. It's a short, clipped "**bap**."

Now, for the culture. The word bap has two meanings. It literally means "steamed rice," but it also means "a meal" in general. Why? Because for centuries in Korea, a meal wasn't considered a proper meal without its heart and soul: a bowl of steamed rice.

This brings us to one of the most common greetings you'll hear in Korea: "밥 먹었어? (**bap meogeosseo?**)"

Literally, this translates to "Did you eat?" To an outsider, it sounds like a random question. But in Korea, it's a classic way of saying, "How are you? I care about you." In a country with a history of hardship, asking if someone has eaten is the most fundamental way to check on their well-being.

This might feel strange, but think about the American greeting, "**What's up?**" Literally, it's asking what is happening or what is in the sky above you. But does anyone ever respond by looking up and listing the things they see? Of course not. The real function of "What's up?" isn't to get information. It's a social code that means, "Hi, I see you, let's acknowledge each other." It's a conversational handshake.

This is the exact same logic behind "밥 먹었어?". The literal question is about food, but the real question is, "I was thinking of you, and I hope you're doing well." It's a greeting packed with history, affection, and a deep sense of community care.

So, when you hear about bap in a K-drama, remember: it's never just about rice. It's about life, affection, and the simple, powerful act of caring for one another.

The "Let's Grab a Meal" Mystery

(밥 한번 먹자)

You're watching a K-drama. Two characters who just had a great first meeting are saying goodbye. One of them smiles brightly and says, "다음에 **밥 한번 먹자** (daeume **bap hanbeon meokja**)!" The subtitle reads, "Let's grab a meal sometime!" You think, "Great! Date #2 is in the bag."

And then... crickets. Weeks go by. They bump into each other again, and the cycle repeats. What went wrong?

Welcome, my friend, to the beautiful, confusing world of the "meal invitation." This phrase is perhaps the most common, socially-accepted, non-binding contract in all of Korea.

The best way to understand it is to compare it to the English phrase, "We should totally hang out sometime!" It's a phrase loaded with good intentions, but it's not a concrete plan. It's a social placeholder, a warm way of saying, "I like you, I enjoyed this interaction, and I'm open to seeing you again in the theoretical future."

This all comes down to a core Korean concept called **밥정 (bap-jeong)**. It's the idea that a special bond and affection (정, jeong) is formed through the simple act of sharing meals (밥, bap) together. In Korea, eating isn't just about food; it's the primary way to build relationships. So, offering to share a meal is a way of saying, "I value our connection."

The mystery, then, is figuring out *which* kind of invitation it is.

1. **The Polite Farewell:** This is the "We should hang out!" version. You'll see this between colleagues or new acquaintances. The key is the vague response. If the other person just smiles and says "네, 좋아요! (Ne, joayo! - Yes, that sounds good!)" without suggesting a date, it was likely a polite goodbye.

2. **The Relationship Test:** In a "sseom" or early dating scenario, this phrase is a probe. One person lobs the "Let's grab a meal" grenade, and the other's response determines everything.

A vague "yes" means they're not that interested. An enthusiastic, "Really? When are you
free?" means the relationship is a go.

3. **The Genuine Invitation:** This is when the phrase
   is backed by real intent. It's often used to offer
   deep comfort or have a serious conversation.
   The clearest proof of this is found in the drama
   known to international fans as **[Something in
   the Rain; 2018, Netflix]**. But here's a fascinating
   cultural secret hidden in plain sight: the original
   Korean title is completely different. It's 밥 잘
   사주는 예쁜 누나 (Bap jal sa-ju-neun ye-ppeun
   nu-na).

This literally translates to "**The Pretty Noona Who
Buys Me Meals Often.**"

That's right—the entire premise of the romance, the
core concept of showing affection through buying
meals, is right there in the original title! While the international title captures the poetic mood of the series,
the Korean title tells you exactly what cultural code this
chapter is all about. The plot is a masterclass in how
the simple act of "grabbing a meal" transforms from
a casual gesture of care into the very language of love.

In the beginning, the female lead, Yoon Jin-ah (Son Ye-jin), buys meals for the male lead, Seo Joon-hee (Jung Hea-in), because he is her best friend's "kid brother." It's an act of casual, familial care—a duty. But as her feelings for him change, so does the meaning of the meal. The simple act of "grabbing a meal" becomes a secret excuse to see each other, evolving into a series of heart-fluttering, clandestine dates. The key turning point comes when he starts insisting on paying. It's not about the money; it's a powerful declaration that he is no longer a kid brother to be taken care of, but a man who wants to be her equal partner. In this drama, who buys the meal, where they eat, and what they talk about becomes the primary, unspoken language of their entire love story. This is bap-jeong in its purest form.

So, the next time you hear "Let's grab a meal," don't just listen to the words. Read the air, check the calendar, and see if a date is actually made. You'll know then if it was just a nice goodbye or the start of something more.

But you don't have to just passively wait and wonder. There are active ways to decode the true intention behind this famously ambiguous phrase. Let's add the right plays to your social playbook.

The DECODER'S Playbook

You've learned the theory behind the "meal invitation." Here are the three essential plays to figure out if it's a real plan or just a polite pleasantry.

Play #1: The "Vague vs. Specific" Test

The Pro-Tip: This is the ultimate litmus test. After someone says, "Let's grab a meal sometime," listen carefully to what happens next. Is it followed by a specific suggestion like, "How about next Friday?" or "What kind of food do you like?" If yes, congratulations, it's a real invitation. If it's just met with a friendly smile and a wave goodbye, it was most likely a pleasantry (인사치레, insachire).

Play #2: The "Counter-Offer" Play

The Pro-Tip: If you genuinely want to see the person again, you don't have to just wait. You can make a move. When they say, "Let's grab a meal sometime," you can respond with a cheerful, "I'd love to! Are you free sometime next week?" Their reaction to your specific proposal will give you a definitive answer. If they commit, it's real. If they give a vague excuse, you know it was just a nice gesture. This play puts you in the driver's seat.

Play #3: The "Read the Room" Play

The Pro-Tip: Context is everything. Who is saying it, and in what situation? A business acquaintance at the end of a meeting? It's likely a polite formality. A close friend who knows you're going through a tough time? It's almost certainly a genuine offer of comfort and support. The closer the existing relationship, the more sincere the invitation usually is.

⬆ Level-Up Vocabulary

약속 (Yaksok, yak-sok) A promise; an appointment; a plan. This is the key to the entire mystery. The question is: was "Let's grab a meal" a real yaksok or not? In K-dramas, a character breaking a yaksok is a serious offense, while another character remembering a small, casually made yaksok is a huge romantic gesture.

한턱내다 (Hanteok-naeda, han-tuk-nae-da) To treat someone (to a meal or drinks); to pay for everything. This is an active and very generous offer. When a character gets a promotion or has good news, they'll often declare to their friends, "**내가 한턱쏠게!** (Naega hanteok-ssolge!)"—"I'll treat you all! / This one's on me!" This is a celebratory phrase that always leads to a fun meal scene.

맛집 (Matjip, maht-jip) A "delicious house"; a famous or popular restaurant known for great food. This is a huge part of modern Korean culture. If a meal invitation is serious, the conversation will often turn to, "**어디 맛집 알아**? (Eodi matjip ara?)"—"Do you know any good restaurants?" Finding a great matjip is a common K-drama date activity.

인사치레 (Insachire, in-sa-chi-reh) Lip service; a polite pleasantry; something said out of courtesy. This word perfectly describes the function of a non-committal "Let's grab a meal." It's not a lie, but rather a social nicety—a way to end a conversation warmly without making a firm promise. Understanding insachire is a high-level social skill.

빈말 (Binmal, bin-mahl) Empty words; an insincere comment. This is a bit more direct and negative than insachire. While insachire is about being polite, binmal implies that the words were said with no real meaning behind them at all. If a character says, "**그거 빈말 아니지**? (Geugeo binmal aniji?)"—"Those weren't just empty words, were they?"—they're asking for genuine reassurance.

 **A Quick Pronunciation Tip for Chapter 8**

This chapter's key term is a delicious one: 반찬 (**ban-chan**). This means "side dishes."

☑ 반 (**ban**): Remember the 안 (an) sound? This is the same, just with a b in front. Say "bahn."

☑ 찬 (**chan**): Sounds like the first part of "**Chan**el" or a "**chan**ce."

Easy, right? **Bahn-chan**. Now you know what to ask for at a Korean restaurant.

The Side-Dish Invasion

(남의 밥그릇에 반찬 올려주기)

You're at a dinner table in a K-drama. The characters are happily eating. Suddenly, one person reaches over with their chopsticks, picks up a piece of glistening kimchi or grilled meat, and places it directly onto another person's bowl of rice.

There's no warning. No "Do you want some?" It's a swift, silent maneuver. Your first thought might be, "Hey, that's my rice! What's happening?"

It's not an attack. It's not a mistake. It's an invasion—a Side-Dish Invasion. And in Korea, it's one of the most powerful non-verbal ways to say, "I care about you."

This single act is the physical manifestation of 정 (Jeong)—that deep, untranslatable Korean concept of affection, connection, and community. It's a gesture that can hold a dozen different meanings depending on the context. It might be a parent silently telling their child, "You're my favorite," or a friend saying, "This is delicious, you have to try it."

Think of it this way: in many Western cultures, the ultimate act of food-sharing intimacy might be letting someone have a bite from your fork. The Side-Dish Invasion is the Korean equivalent, but it's even more common and woven into the fabric of everyday meals. It's a casual act of service and a clear sign of an established bond.

This code is a language spoken fluently in almost every K-drama.

In [응답하라 1988, **Reply 1988; 2015, Netflix/Viki]**, the dinner table is the main stage for this. The neighborhood moms are constantly—almost aggressively—placing side dishes onto the bowls of their own kids, their friends' kids, and anyone who looks like they need a little extra love. It's the ultimate expression of a mother's (and a community's) desire to see you well-fed and cared for.

The gesture becomes even more significant in a romantic context. In [사랑의 불시착, **Crash Landing on You; 2019, Netflix]**, Captain Ri Jeong-hyeok isn't a man of many words. Instead, he shows his growing affection for Yoon Se-ri through actions. When he grills meat to perfection and places the best piece on her spoon or in her bowl, he's saying what he can't yet verbalize: "I'm looking out for you. You are special to me."

So don't be fooled. That little piece of kimchi landing in your bowl isn't just food. It's a Trojan horse, and it's smuggling in a massive amount of affection, care, and Jeong. So, what's the right way to react to this delicious invasion? Just smile, and eat well. Mission accomplished.

Now that you can read this silent conversation, how should you respond when you're a part of it? Knowing the right moves is key. Let's add the essential plays to your dining playbook.

🔍 The **DECODER'S** Playbook

You understand the beautiful meaning behind the Side-Dish Invasion. Here are the three key plays for handling this gesture with grace.

Play #1: The "Accept and Enjoy" Play

The Pro-Tip: This is the most important rule for the receiver. If someone—especially an elder, a parent figure, or your boss—places a side dish onto your bowl, the correct and only response is to receive it with gratitude. Smile, give a slight nod or bow of the head, and eat it well. Refusing the food would be seen as rejecting their affection (정, jeong) and could be quite rude. Just enjoy the gesture of care.

Play #2: The "Know Your Target" Play

The Pro-Tip: Thinking of initiating a Side-Dish Invasion yourself? First, consider your relationship with the other person. This gesture is most common and welcomed between family members and very close friends. While it can be a romantic move in a Sseom situation, doing it too early with a new acquaintance might come across as overly familiar. When in doubt, it's safer to just recommend a side dish ("You should try this, it's delicious!") rather than placing it in their bowl directly.

Play #3: The "Affection Exchange" Play

The Pro-Tip: This is the advanced move. If a close friend or partner places their favorite banchan on your bowl, a great way to respond is by reciprocating later in the meal. Find a side dish you particularly enjoy and put it in their bowl. This turns a one-way gesture of care into a two-way exchange, a visible sign of a strong and reciprocal friendship.

⬆ Level-Up Vocabulary

챙겨주다 (Chaeng-gyeo-juda, chaeng-gyuh-joo-da)
To take care of someone; to look out for someone. This verb describes the thoughtful, often unsolicited, acts of service for someone you care about. The act of a mother putting her son's favorite side dish on his rice is a perfect example of **챙겨주다 (chaeng-gyeo-juda)**.

애정 표현 (Aejeong pyohyeon, ae-jung-pyo-hyun) An expression of affection. This is the core function of the Side-Dish Invasion. In a culture where direct "I love you"s can sometimes be considered embarrassing or too dramatic, small gestures like this become a crucial aejeong pyohyeon. It's a way to show love without having to say a word.

다정하다 (Dajeonghada, da-jung-ha-da) To be sweet, kind, or affectionate. This adjective describes the personality of a person who frequently initiates a Side-Dish Invasion. In K-dramas, the "sweet second lead"—the kind and caring second male lead who never gets the girl—is often shown as being very dajeonghada, taking care of the main character by making sure they're eating well.

 **A Quick Pronunciation Tip for Chapter 9**

This chapter's keyword is 썸 (**sseom**), and its pronunciation is key.

☑ ㅆ (**ss**): This is a "tense" or "sharp" 's' sound. To make it, place your tongue as if you're about to say "s," but create more tension and force the air out in a short, strong burst. It's a hissy sound, like a "s-s-snake."

☑ 어 (**eo**): The relaxed vowel, like the 'u' in "sun."

☑ ㅁ (**m**): Just a simple 'm' sound at the end.

Put it all together: **ss-uh-m** ➜ **sseom**.

The Art of "Sseom"

(썸)

You're watching two K-drama characters who are definitely more than friends. They text each other all night about nothing. They "accidentally" brush hands and then act flustered for ten minutes. He knows her exact coffee order, and she knows his favorite movie.

So, they're dating, right? Nope.

Welcome, my friend, to the deliciously frustrating, heart-pounding, unofficial relationship stage known as 썸 (**sseom**).

If you've ever been in a "situationship," you already understand **Sseom**. The word itself is pure genius, born from the English word "**some**thing." As in, "There's *something* between us... but it's not *anything* official yet." It's the gray area, the "are we or aren't we?" limbo that fuels 90% of all romantic comedies.

Sseom is a high-stakes game of emotional chicken. It has its own unwritten rules: You can be jealous, but you have no official right to be. You can expect a "good morning" text, but you can't get mad if it doesn't come. This phase is all about 밀당 (**mildang**)—a strategic game of push-and-pull. It's maddening. It's thrilling. It's the essence of K-drama romance.

Imagine this: You start frequenting a coffee shop near your place, mostly because the cute barista has a great playlist. After a few visits, he starts remembering your order. One day, he draws a tiny, winking smiley face next to your name on the cup. The next week, you find each other on Instagram. Soon, you're replying to each other's stories at 2 AM. Your friends start asking, "So... what's the deal with the cute barista?" You don't know what to say, because you don't know either.

Congratulations. That barista? He is your 썸남 (**sseom-nam**)—the guy you have "something" with. To him, you are his 썸녀 (**sseom-nyeo**). And this whole confusing, heart-fluttering process? That is called 썸 타다 (**sseom-tada**)—literally, "to ride the something."

No drama explores the seductive danger of modern Sseom quite like [알고있지만, **Nevertheless; 2021, Netflix**]. It is the ultimate masterclass on the topic. Think of the iconic scene where the male lead, Park Jae-eon, meets the female lead, Yoo Na-bi, for the first time in a bar. Instead of asking for her number, he gently takes her arm and draws a butterfly—her name, Na-bi, means butterfly—on her skin. It's an intensely intimate, heart-stopping gesture, but it comes with zero commitment. That single act *is* Sseom: thrilling, artistic, and beautifully ambiguous.

But Sseom isn't always a minefield. For a sweeter version, look at [역도요정 김복주, **Weightlifting Fairy Kim Bok-joo; 2016, Viki/Netflix**]. The journey of the two leads from bickering best friends to something more is full of heart-fluttering Sseom moments. Even a more mature drama like [사랑의 이해, **The Interest of Love; 2022, Netflix**] explores how getting stuck in the Sseom phase for too long can lead to years of painful what-ifs.

So, Sseom is the phase of pure potential. It's the "will they or won't they?" stretched out over several episodes, packed with longing stares and near-miss kisses. It's the thrilling, uncertain "something" right before it becomes a definite everything.

And you simply can't talk about Sseom without mentioning the mega-hit song: **"Some(썸)" by Soyou and Junggigo (2014)**. This song, which wasn't a drama OST, perfectly captured the frustrating but heart-fluttering lyrics of a modern Sseom ("It feels like you're mine, but not... It feels like I'm yours, but not..."). It became the official anthem for everyone "riding the something," and solidified the term Sseom in the Korean language forever.

Navigating that uncertain "something" can feel like walking a tightrope without a net. So how do you keep your balance and make it to the other side? Let's add the essential survival plays to your playbook.

The **DECODER'S** Playbook

You've learned the definition of the heart-fluttering Sseom. Here are the three key plays to survive—and win—this ambiguous game.

Play #1: The "Pattern Detective" Play

The Pro-Tip: Is it real Sseom or are they just being friendly? Stop focusing on a single moment and become a pattern detective. One late-night text could be a fluke. Consistent late-night texting is a pattern. One "accidental" hand brush is an accident. Three of them, combined with remembering your coffee order? That's data. Look for a consistent pattern of special attention. That's your most reliable clue.

Play #2: The "Decode the Push-Pull" Play

The Pro-Tip: The most confusing part of Sseom is the 밀당 (**mildang**) (push-pull). They seem super interested one day, then slightly distant the next. Don't panic! This is often a test to gauge your interest. If they "push" (pull back slightly) and you react with a little jealousy or show you miss them, you're signaling that you're invested. Understanding this game helps you not to overthink every little "push."

Play #3: The "Break the Cycle" Play

The Pro-Tip: Sseom can't last forever. If the ambiguity is driving you crazy, one person has to be brave. This is the 고백 **(gobaek)** (confession) play. It's a high-risk, high-reward move, but it's the only way to end the game and find out if you can level up to an official couple (사귀다, sagwida). So what's the ultimate cheat code to break free from that "what are we?" limbo? It's the same in K-dramas as it is in real life: a clear, honest confession.

⬆ Level-Up Vocabulary

밀당 (**Mildang, mil-dang**) Push-pull. This is the core strategy and the art form within any 썸 (sseom). It's a strategic game of showing interest (pull) and then acting aloof (push) to keep the other person on their toes and make them more interested. K-drama characters are masters of mildang, agonizing for hours over when to reply to a text to seem cool but not cold.

고백하다 (**Gobaekhada, go-baek-ha-da**) To confess (one's romantic feelings). This is the decisive quest-ender for any sseom. The 고백 (gobaek) is the dramatic, high-stakes moment when one person finally puts their cards on the table and says, "I like you." This confession is what officially turns a sseom into a real relationship... or ends it completely.

사귀다 (**Sagwida, sa-gwi-da**) To date; to be in a relationship; to "go out." This is the official status you achieve after a successful sseom and 고백 (gobaek).

When characters ask, "우리 오늘부터 1일이야? (Uri oneul-buteo iril-iya?)"—"Is today our Day 1?"—they are confirming that they are now officially a couple. It marks the end of ambiguity.

애매하다 (Aemaehada, ae-mae-ha-da) To be vague, ambiguous, or uncertain. This adjective is the perfect word to describe the state of sseom. Is he just being friendly, or does he like me? Is she just replying to be polite, or is she interested? This aemaehan (ambiguous) feeling is what makes the sseom phase both so thrilling and so frustrating.

어장관리 (Eojang-gwanli, uh-jang-gwan-lee) Literally "fish farm management." This is a brilliant piece of modern slang for the dark side of sseom. It describes the act of keeping multiple potential romantic interests (썸남 (sseom-nam) and 썸녀 (sseom-nyeo)) on the hook without committing to any of them, just like a farmer managing their fish. In a drama, when a character is texting several people flirtatiously, they're often accused of eojang-gwanli.

 **A Quick Pronunciation Tip for Chapter 10**

This chapter is about Korea's most famous drink: 소주 (**so-ju**).

☑ 소 (**so**): Sounds exactly like the English word "**so**" (as in, "I love this drama so much!").

☑ 주 (**ju**): Sounds like the name "**Ju**" in "**Ju**ly" or "**Ju**dy."

That's it: **So-ju**. Now you're ready for a virtual drink.

Decoding the Green Bottle

(초록병 암호 해독하기)

In any K-drama, there's a supporting character who shows up more often than a meddling mother-in-law or a surprise chaebol heir. It's small, green, and holds within it the secrets to Korean social dynamics. We're talking, of course, about the iconic green bottle of 소주 (**so-ju**).

When you see characters gathered around a table with this bottle, don't just watch them drink. Watch how they drink. You're about to witness a complex and fascinating ritual, a physical performance where every gesture is a line of code, revealing respect, hierarchy, and intimacy.

Think of it like the unwritten rules of a very formal dinner party in the West—knowing which fork to use, when to stand up, who speaks first. The soju table has its own grammar, and we're about to give you the cheat sheet.

Here are the core codes you need to crack to master the art of the green bottle:

Code #1: The Two-Handed Rule (Respect in Your Hands)

- This is the golden rule. When pouring for an elder or a senior (like your boss), you must use two hands—either by holding the bottle with both hands, or by using your right hand to pour while your left hand gently supports your right wrist or elbow. The same applies when receiving a drink from them. It's a physical sign of respect that says, "You are important, and I honor your status."

Code #2: The Head Turn (Averting Your Gaze)

- After receiving a drink from a senior, a character will almost always turn their head slightly to the side (away from the senior) to drink it. It's considered polite to not show yourself drinking directly in front of an elder. This subtle gesture is another powerful sign of deference and respect.

Code #3: The Empty Glass Rule (Never Let It Be Empty, Never Pour for Yourself)

- At a Korean drinking table, your glass is everyone else's responsibility but your own. It's considered good manners to keep an eye on your companions' glasses, especially a senior's, and refill it when it's empty. Inversely, pouring your own drink is a social faux pas. This rule transforms drinking from an individual act into a communal one, constantly reinforcing the group's bond.

These codes are brilliantly showcased in the classic office drama [미생, **Misaeng: Incomplete Life; 2014, Netflix**]. Think of the excruciatingly awkward company dinners (회식, hwesik) that the newly-joined intern, Jang Geu-rae, is essentially dragged to. He knows no one, he doesn't understand the corporate hierarchy, and he's surrounded by his intimidating superiors. It's a scenario that gives anyone social anxiety. The camera masterfully focuses on his nervous hands as he tries to pour soju for his boss with two hands, his eyes darting around, terrified of leaving a glass empty. For him, every gesture is a high-stakes test, and this drinking session isn't a party—it's his first, most confusing, and most important exam on Korean corporate culture.

You can also see the emotional weight of these rituals in [이태원 클라쓰, **Itaewon Class; 2020, Netflix**]. There's a powerful scene in the very first episode where Park Sae-ro-yi's father teaches him how to properly receive a drink for the first time. This isn't just a lesson about alcohol; it's a father passing down the codes of respect and adulthood to his son. For a more casual but equally insightful look, [술꾼도시여자들, **Work Later Drink Now; 2021, TVING**] shows how these rules are adapted and playfully bent among close friends.

So, the green bottle isn't just a prop. It's a social tool. And now that you know the code, you'll be able to read the entire power dynamic of a room just by watching who turns their head and who uses two hands.

Reading the room is a great skill. But what happens when that green bottle is passed to you? Don't panic. This isn't a test; it's a team sport. Here are the plays to make you a valuable team player.

The **DECODER'S** Playbook

You've decoded the rules of the green bottle. Here are the four most important plays to navigate a real-life Korean drinking session (술자리, `suljari`) with style and respect.

Play #1: The "Pacing is Everything" Play

The Pro-Tip: Do you have to `wonshot` (bottoms up) every glass? Absolutely not. A good strategy is to match the pace of your superiors for the first one or two glasses as a sign of respect. After that, it's perfectly okay to slow down. A secret tip? If you want to avoid getting your glass refilled too often, always keep it about half-full. People are less likely to top up a glass that isn't empty.

Play #2: The "Strategic Water" Play

The Pro-Tip: What if you can't or don't want to drink alcohol? Don't just refuse the drink; participate in the ritual. Politely tell your senior that you don't drink and ask for a glass of water or soda instead. Then, when everyone does a `geonbae` (cheers), you raise your glass of water and participate in the toast. This shows you respect the group activity, even if you're not drinking the alcohol.

Play #3: The "Proactive Junior" Play

The Pro-Tip: Want to impress your Korean boss? Don't just wait for their glass to be empty. When a new bottle of soju is opened, be the one to proactively take the bottle and offer to pour the first glass for the most senior person at the table. This shows you're not just passively following rules, but actively contributing to the positive atmosphere of the hoesik. It's a guaranteed way to be seen as a thoughtful and sensible junior.

Play #4: The "Know Your Limits" Play

The Pro-Tip: Korean drinking culture can be intense, but you are not obligated to keep up with a heavy drinker (주당, **judang**). If you're feeling overwhelmed, it is perfectly acceptable to politely signal your limits. You can say, **"저는 주량이 약해서요 (Jeoneun juryang-i yak-haeseoyo)**"—"My alcohol tolerance is weak." It's a polite and effective way to manage your pace without offending anyone.

⬆ Level-Up Vocabulary

회식 (Hoesik, hwe-shik) A company dinner. This is the primary stage for the soju rituals in K-dramas. A **hoesik** isn't just a casual meal with colleagues; it's an extension of the workplace, often mandatory, where team bonding (and a lot of drama) happens. It's where you'll see rookies nervously pouring soju for their bosses and where secret office romances are often accidentally revealed.

건배 (Geonbae, gun-bae) / 짠 (Jjan, jjan) Cheers! Geonbae is the standard, more formal word for "cheers." However, you'll more often hear the much more casual and cute-sounding 짠 **(jjan)**! Jjan is the sound of glasses clinking together, and it's the go-to cheer among friends and younger people.

원샷 (Wonshot, won-shat) One-shot; bottoms up. A classic Konglish term. When the mood is high, characters will often chant to encourage someone to drink their entire glass of soju in one go. You'll often hear them shout, "**원샷해! (Wonshot-hae!)**"—"Bottoms up!"

주량 (**Juryang, joo-ryang**) Drinking capacity; alcohol tolerance. A person's juryang is a frequent topic of conversation. A character with a high juryang is often seen as strong or cool, while a character with a low juryang is the one who will inevitably get drunk and cause trouble or spill a major secret.

술버릇 (**Sulbeoreut, sool-buh-reut**) Drinking habits; what a person does when they're drunk. A character's **sulbeoreut** is a major plot device in K-dramas. It can be cute (like becoming extra affectionate) or dramatic (like revealing a hidden truth). It's the "truth serum" of the K-drama world. It is also sometimes called 주사 (**jusa**), which often refers to more problematic or extreme drunken habits.

2차 (**I-cha, ee-cha**) Second round. The drinking in K-dramas rarely ends after just dinner. I-cha is the second round, which could be at another bar, a Korean-style karaoke bar (노래방, noraebang), or a chicken-and-beer place. If the night goes on, you might even hear them plan a 3차 (sam-cha), or third round. It shows a commitment to a long night of bonding.

해장 (Hae-jang, hae-jang) The essential ritual of curing a hangover. Haejang is the Korean art of chasing away a hangover (숙취, sukchwi) by eating a bubbling, often spicy, "hangover soup" (해장국, haejangguk). You'll see characters, looking exhausted, huddled over a hot bowl and saying, "**아, 시원하다 (Ah, si-won-ha-da)**"—a phrase that ironically means "Ah, that's refreshing," which is what Koreans say when consuming something deeply satisfying, like a hot soup. It's the final, necessary chapter of any proper Korean drinking night.

PART 3

The Life Code
(일상 속에 숨겨진 문화)

A bowl of seaweed soup on a birthday. A messy plate of black bean noodles on moving day. A white sheet mask at the end of a long day. A casual get-together at a brightly lit convenience store.

In K-dramas, these aren't just random quirks or plot devices. They are a language in themselves. They are the Life Code.

If Part 1 was about decoding what Koreans say, and Part 2 was about decoding how they relate, then this final part is about decoding how they *live*. It's about the everyday rituals and the symbolic meanings of the places and foods that make up the very fabric of their world.

Think of this final part of the book as the master key. Once you understand the life codes, you won't just understand the characters' actions; you'll understand their world.

Ready to finally understand not just *what* they do, but *why* they do it?

The magic of everyday life and love in *Hometown Cha-Cha-Cha*

 **A Quick Pronunciation Tip for Chapter 11**

Let's learn the star of our moving day feast: 짜장면
(jja-jang-myeon).

☑️ 짜 (jja): This is a tense consonant, with no puff
of air. To make the sound, place your tongue as
if you're about to say "ju**dg**e," but tense up your
tongue and release the sound in a short, sharp
burst. It's a tight sound, like a quick "**jya**."

☑️ 장 (jang): Easy! Sounds like "**jahng**."

☑️ 면 (myeon): Combine "mee" (like "see me") and
"yun." So, "**mee-yun**," quickly blended.

Put it all together: **Jja-jahng-mee-yun** ➡️ **Jja-jang-
myeon**. Delicious just saying it!

Jjajangmyeon Moving Day!

(이사하면 짜장면이지!)

There's an unwritten law in South Korea, a rule so powerful it governs even the most chaotic of days: moving day. The rule is simple. Before a single box is truly unpacked, before the furniture is arranged, you must sit on the floor, surrounded by your best friends, and order a glorious, messy bowl of **짜장면 (jja-jang-myeon)**.

If you're not Korean, your first thought might be, "Why **jjajangmyeon**? Why not Korean BBQ or celebratory fried chicken?"

The answer is a delicious blend of practicality, nostalgia, and a touch of Korean history. In the bustling process of moving, surrounded by chaos, the last thing anyone wants to do is cook. Jjajangmyeon is the perfect moving-day fuel because it's fast, delivered right to your doorstep, easy to eat communally on the floor, and affordable.

But the tradition goes deeper than just convenience. Jjajangmyeon holds a special place in the hearts of many Koreans, often associated with happy occasions and a sense of simple comfort. Think of it as Korea's ultimate comfort food that happens to be logistically perfect for a moving day.

This tradition is deeply embedded in Korean pop culture. You can see it beautifully in the very first episode of [응답하라 1988, Reply 1988; 2015, Netflix/Viki], when Deok-sun's family moves into the Ssangmun-dong neighborhood. Amidst the chaos of unpacked boxes, they share their first meal of jjajangmyeon with their new neighbors, instantly forming a bond over the messy, delicious bowls.

And if [Reply 1988] shows the tradition's heartwarming roots, [스타트업, Start-Up; 2020, Netflix] shows its modern, chaotic evolution. As a volatile startup, the Samsan Tech team moves offices multiple times, and their celebratory ritual each time is—you guessed it—jjajangmyeon. You can see them christening their new beginnings with black bean noodles in both Episode 5 and Episode 11, making it the official fuel of their rollercoaster journey from underdogs to champions.

Even in more recent dramas, the tradition persists, a nod to a beloved cultural norm. The simple act of eating jjajangmyeon on moving day is a visual shorthand that tells viewers: "This is a new chapter, and we're facing it together." It's a delicious and heartwarming tradition that perfectly captures the spirit of starting fresh.

Now that you understand the "why," let's get into the "how." Whether you're the one moving or the one helping a friend, here are the key plays to make any moving day deliciously successful.

The **DECODER'S** Playbook

You've learned why `jjajangmyeon` is the official moving day meal. Here are the three essential plays to participate in this tradition like a seasoned pro.

Play #1: The "Don't Cook, Just Call" Play

The Pro-Tip: Your friend is moving, and you want to help? The number one rule is: do not offer to cook. The beauty of the jjajangmyeon tradition lies in its convenience amidst the chaos. The most helpful thing you can do is grab your phone, find the nearest 중국집 (`junggukjip`), and confidently say, "I'll handle the food!" This shows you truly understand the culture.

Play #2: The "Mix Vigorously, Slurp Loudly" Play

The Pro-Tip: The delivery has arrived. Your `jjajangmyeon` is in front of you. What's the right way to eat it? First, you must mix the noodles and the black bean sauce vigorously. This essential act is called 비비다 (`bibida`) in Korean, and the goal is to make sure the sauce coats every strand of the noodles perfectly. Second, don't be afraid to slurp! In Korea, slurping your noodles is not rude; it's a sign that you are thoroughly enjoying your meal. Don't forget to eat the bright yellow pickled radish (단무지, `danmuji`) in between bites for the perfect flavor balance.

Play #3: The "Housewarming Gift" Play

The Pro-Tip: The moving day jjajangmyeon is a casual affair for the helpers. The real celebration is the housewarming party (집들이, `jipdeuri`) that happens later. When you're invited to that, you should bring a gift. The traditional, symbolic gifts are toilet paper (휴지, `hyuji`) and laundry detergent (세제, `seje`). The long, unrolling toilet paper symbolizes the wish that all the homeowner's problems will "unravel" smoothly, while the bubbles from the detergent symbolize the wish for wealth and prosperity to "bubble up." It's a practical and meaningful gift.

⬆ Level-Up Vocabulary

이사 (Isa, ee-sa) Moving; the act of moving houses. This is the main event that triggers the 짜장면 (jjajangmyeon) tradition. In K-dramas, an isa scene is a visual shorthand for a new start, a change in fortune, or the beginning of a new chapter in a character's life.

배달 (Baedal, bae-dal) Delivery. Korea has an incredibly advanced and fast delivery culture, and baedal is at the heart of the moving day tradition. The ability to get hot, delicious food delivered to a messy, chaotic apartment with just one phone call is what makes jjajangmyeon the perfect choice. When you hear a character shout, **"배달 왔습니다! (Baedal wasseumnida!)"** ("Delivery's here!"), it's a sound of pure joy.

중국집 (Junggukjip, joong-gook-jip) A Korean-style Chinese restaurant. This is where the magic happens. Junggukjip are the restaurants that specialize in Korean-Chinese fusion food, with jjajangmyeon being their star player. They are famous for their lightning-fast baedal service.

단무지 **(Danmuji, dahn-moo-jee)** Yellow pickled radish. This is the one and only side dish (반찬, banchan) that is considered the soulmate of jjajangmyeon. It's bright yellow, sweet, sour, and crunchy. No jjajangmyeon meal is complete without a side of danmuji. It's a non-negotiable part of the package.

집들이 **(Jipdeuri, jip-deu-ree)** A housewarming party. This is the official event that often happens a few days or weeks after the isa (moving day). While moving day is for close friends eating jjajangmyeon on the floor, the jipdeuri is a more formal party where the new homeowner invites friends and family to show off their new place and treats them to a home-cooked meal. A classic K-drama trope is a character agonizing over what to bring as a jipdeuri gift.

 **A Quick Pronunciation Tip for Chapter 12**

Today's special menu is 미역국 (`mi-yeok-guk`)! Let's get it right.

☑ 미 (`mi`): Sounds just like the English word "**me**."

☑ 역 (`yeok`): This one is tricky. It's a combination of yeo (like the 'u' in "sun") and a k sound at the end. But the k is soft, almost silent. Think of saying "**yuh**" and then just stopping the sound with the back of your tongue.

☑ 국 (`guk`): Sounds like the word "**cook,**" but the 'k' at the end is also soft and unreleased. Just gently close the back of your throat to end the sound.

It's a mouthful, but you'll get it: **Mee-yuhk-cook**.

CHAPTER Twelve

Seaweed Soup for Birthdays!

(생일엔 미역국!)

It's a K-drama character's birthday. The cake is ready, and the presents are wrapped, but the celebration can't truly begin until they've had... a bowl of seaweed soup. Not exactly the festive party food you were expecting, right? It's not sweet, it's not bubbly, and it doesn't come with candles.

So why is this humble, savory soup the undisputed star of every Korean birthday?

The answer is a beautiful tradition that connects every birthday back to the person who made it possible: your mother.

Here's the cultural code: Seaweed (미역, miyeok) is incredibly rich in calcium and iodine, nutrients that are crucial for a mother recovering from childbirth. For centuries, it has been a Korean tradition for new mothers to eat 미역국 (miyeokguk) for weeks after giving birth to help their bodies heal and to produce nutritious milk for their newborn.

So, eating seaweed soup on your birthday isn't really about you. It's a deeply meaningful ritual. It's a way of honoring your mother, remembering the pain and love of your own birth, and expressing gratitude for the gift of life. It's a culinary "thank you" note to your mom.

This tradition is a powerful source of emotion in K-dramas.

- **A Symbol of Love & Care:** When a mother, grandmother, or even a romantic partner lovingly prepares miyeokguk for someone's birthday, it's a profound act of care. In [**갯마을 차차차, Hometown Cha-Cha-Cha; 2021, Netflix]**, this tradition shows the power of a chosen family. The town's grandmothers make miyeokguk for the orphaned Chief Hong, acting as his surrogate mothers. The tradition takes on a romantic meaning later, when the chic city dentist, Yoon Hye-jin, awkwardly fumbles in the kitchen, following a recipe on her phone to make the soup for him. For a character like her, this act of learning and cooking a traditional, time-consuming dish is a far greater declaration of love than any expensive gift.

- **A Symbol of Loneliness:** Conversely, a character spending their birthday alone without a bowl of miyeokguk is a powerful visual for sadness and neglect. The most heartbreaking example is in [도깨비, **Goblin; 2016, Viki**]. In Episode 2, the orphaned heroine, Ji Eun-tak, has to cook her own sad, single-serving miyeokguk on her 19th birthday. It instantly tells us everything about her lonely life. The emotional payoff comes in Episode 10, when the hero, Kim Shin, prepares a proper, warm birthday feast for her—including **miyeokguk**. This act signifies that she has finally found a new family and someone who will remember and cherish the day she was born.

So, while birthday cake is for the party, seaweed soup is for the heart. It's a simple, powerful tradition that reminds every K-drama character (and us!) that every celebration of life begins with a mother's love.

This tradition is full of heart. So, how can you navigate it with the same level of thoughtfulness? Here are the plays that show you truly understand the meaning behind the soup.

The DECODER'S Playbook

You've learned the beautiful reason behind birthday seaweed soup. Here are the three essential plays to navigate this heartwarming tradition.

Play #1: The "Call Your Mom" Play

The Pro-Tip: This is the most important play. After eating miyeokguk on your birthday, the very first thing you should do is call your mother. The goal isn't just to say "Thanks for the soup." The real purpose is to say, **"낳아주시고 키워주셔서 감사합니다 (Na-a-jusigo ki-wo-jusyeoseo gamsahamnida)"**—"Thank you for giving birth to me and raising me." This act completes the circle of gratitude and is the true heart of the tradition.

Play #2: The "Thoughtful Friend" Play

The Pro-Tip: It's your Korean friend's birthday. What do you do? While a cake and presents are great, asking a simple question like, "미역국 먹었어요? (Miyeokguk meogeosseoyo?)"—"Did you have your seaweed soup?"—shows a deep level of cultural understanding and care. If your friend is living away from their family, offering to cook it for them is one of the most touching gestures of friendship you can make.

Play #3: The "Not for the Party" Play

The Pro-Tip: Remember that `miyeokguk` is not party food. It's a personal, reflective meal, often eaten in the morning with family. You would not serve it at a big birthday bash alongside pizza and beer. The party is for celebrating with friends; the seaweed soup is for a quiet moment of gratitude and honoring one's family. Knowing the difference is a true insider move.

생일 (Saeng-il, saeng-eel) Birthday. The main event! Saeng-il is the day that calls for seaweed soup. In K-dramas, a character's saeng-il is often a major plot point, leading to surprise parties, romantic dates, or sometimes, a lonely and forgotten day that highlights their sadness.

축하하다 (Chukahada, choo-ka-ha-da) To congratulate; to celebrate. The essential action for any birthday. You'll hear the song "생일 축하합니다 (Saeng-il chuka-hamnida)," which is the Korean "Happy Birthday to You." Friends will shout "생일 축하해! (Saeng-il chukahae!)" ("Happy Birthday!") as they bring out the cake.

선물 (Seonmul, sun-mool) A gift; a present. Besides the 미역국 (miyeokguk), seonmul is the other key component of a K-drama birthday. The type of seonmul a character gives is often a huge symbol of their feelings—a thoughtfully chosen, humble gift often means more than an expensive, impersonal one from a rich rival.

어머니 (**Eomeoni, uh-muh-nee**) Mother (formal). This is the key figure in the seaweed soup tradition. While there are more casual words for "mom" (엄마, eomma), eomeoni is a respectful, formal term. Eating miyeokguk on your birthday is a culinary act of remembering and honoring your eomeoni for the hardship of childbirth.

감사 (**Gamsa, gahm-sa**) Gratitude; thanks; appreciation. This is the core emotion of the birthday tradition. You express gamsa for the presents and the party, but the bowl of seaweed soup represents a deeper gamsa towards your parents for the gift of life itself. It's the unspoken "thank you" in every spoonful.

 **A Quick Pronunciation Tip for Chapter 13**

This chapter has two keywords that are a perfect pair: 금수저 (geum-su-jeo) and 흙수저 (heuk-su-jeo).

☑ 금 (geum): Let's build this sound. It starts with a soft 'g' (like in "**g**o"). The vowel is our tricky friend 으 (eu)—the sound you make when you say "**ugh!**" but without the 'gh'. Finish it with a simple 'm' sound. It's a quick blend: **g-eu-m ➜ geum**.

☑ 흙 (heuk): This one's tough! Start by saying "**huh**," then add a soft, unreleased 'k' sound at the end by closing the back of your throat. It's a quick, single syllable: **heuk**.

☑ 수저 (su-jeo): **soo** + **juh**. Think "**sue-juh**."

You've got it! **Geum-su-jeo** (gold spoon) and **Heuk-su-jeo** (dirt spoon).

The Spoon Class System

(흙수저와 금수저)

You've probably heard the English expression, "born with a silver spoon in one's mouth," right? It means being born into a wealthy, privileged family.

Well, in the high-stakes, ultra-rich world of K-dramas, silver just isn't good enough. They have 금수저 (geum-su-jeo)—the **gold spoon**. This isn't just rich; this is chaebol-level, "I could buy this entire city block if I felt like it" rich. This is the starting line for the characters who seem to have everything: the expensive cars, the designer clothes, and the powerful parents who can make any problem disappear.

The opposite of the gold spoon is the 흙수저 (heuk-su-jeo), which literally translates to the powerful and gritty term 'dirt spoon.' Think of it as the Korean equivalent of being "born on the wrong side of the tracks" or starting "from rags." It's the starting point for every hardworking, underdog K-drama hero we love to root for—the ones living in rooftop apartments, working multiple part-time jobs, and fighting for a chance to prove themselves.

This isn't just a metaphor; it's a modern, informal caste system that many Koreans use to talk about social mobility and inequality. It's called the "Spoon Class System" (수저계급론), and it's the invisible software that runs the plot of countless K-dramas.

Let's be honest, there's a reason why this theme is so incredibly addictive. It taps into our deepest feelings about fairness and justice, offering two powerful emotional payoffs: vicarious satisfaction and catharsis. On one hand, we get a vicarious thrill from the geumsujeo lifestyle—the walk-in closets, the fleets of luxury cars. It's pure escapist fantasy. But the real emotional core, the catharsis, comes from watching the heuksujeo protagonist, through sheer grit and intelligence, finally triumph over the system. We cheer for their success and celebrate their meticulously planned revenge because it feels like a victory for every underdog.

This class warfare is the entire premise of the classic drama [상속자들, **The Heirs; 2013, Netflix/Viki**]. It literally pits the "heirs" (geumsujeo) against the "socially-cared-for" students (heuksujeo) within an elite high school.

You can see the ultimate heuksujeo revenge fantasy in [이태원 클라쓰, **Itaewon Class; 2020, Netflix]**, where Park Sae-ro-yi, a definitive dirt spoon, takes on a massive geumsujeo food conglomerate. This theme is explored with chilling perfection in the Oscar-winning film [기생충, **Parasite; 2019, Hulu/Max]**, where the invisible "smell" of poverty becomes an uncrossable line separating the two families. It's also central to the plot of [더 글로리, **The Glory; 2022, Netflix]**, where the perpetrators' geumsujeo status enables their violence and fuels the victim's lifelong quest for justice. The concept even becomes a literal plot device in the drama [금수저, **The Golden Spoon; 2022, Disney+/Hulu]**, where a magical spoon allows a character to switch lives.

Understanding the Spoon Class System is essential. It's the key that unlocks the core motivation, the desperation, and the ambition that drives so many of your favorite K-drama characters.

Now that you can see this powerful code, you can use it as an analytical tool to understand the plot on a much deeper level. This system isn't just a background detail; it's the playbook for the entire story.

The **DECODER'S** Playbook

You've learned the rules of the Spoon Class System. Here are the key plays to help you analyze any K-drama like a seasoned critic.

Play #1: The "Why Is the Rich Mom ALWAYS So Evil?" Play

The Pro-Tip: It's one of K-drama's greatest mysteries. Why does the mother of geumsujeo (it's almost always the mother) act with such cartoonish villainy, complete with envelopes of money and the infamous water-throwing scene? The secret is that she isn't just a person; she's a symbol. She is the human embodiment of the "Spoon Class System" itself—a walking, designer-bag-wielding wall whose sole purpose is to protect the family's wealth and "purity." Her extreme, often illogical, opposition is a necessary plot device to make the 흙수저 (heuksujeo) protagonist's struggle feel epic and their eventual victory even sweeter.

Play #2: The "Can a Gold Spoon and a Dirt Spoon *Actually* Be Friends?" Play

The Pro-Tip: K-dramas love to test this question. The answer is usually: "Yes, but it's incredibly difficult." In high school, their friendship might seem pure. But as adults, their realities diverge. One worries about next month's rent (월세, wolse); the other worries about a hostile corporate takeover. The friendship can only survive if the geumsujeo character learns to respect the heuksujeo's fierce pride (자존심, jajonsim) and understands that not every problem can be solved by throwing money at it.

Play #3: The "Ultimate Romance Obstacle" Play

The Pro-Tip: The Spoon Class System is the number one obstacle in K-drama romance. The central conflict is almost never just "we can't be together because you're poor." It's more nuanced. It's the disapproving chaebol parent, the clash of values, and the fundamental inability of the rich character to understand the daily struggles of the poor one. The central question of the romance always becomes: "Can love conquer class?"

성공 (Seonggong, sung-gong) Success. This is the ultimate goal of every 흙수저 (heuksujeo) protagonist. In K-dramas, seonggong isn't just about making money; it's about earning respect, proving your worth to those who looked down on you, and gaining the power to protect the ones you love. It's the driving force of the entire plot.

가난 (Ganan, ga-nahn) Poverty. The state that the heuksujeo is desperately trying to escape. K-dramas often portray ganan not just as a lack of money, but as a source of humiliation and powerlessness. This experience is what forges the main character's resilience and unshakeable determination.

부자 (Buja, boo-ja) A rich person. While 금수저 (geumsujeo) refers to a specific class, buja is the more general term for anyone who is wealthy. In a drama, you might hear a character say, "저 사람은 진짜 부자야 (Jeo saram-eun jinjja buja-ya)"—"That person is seriously rich."

복수 (Boksu, bok-soo) Revenge. When the Spoon Class System creates deep injustice, boksu is often the result. Dramas like [이태원 클라쓰, Itaewon Class] or [더 글로리, The Glory] are epic tales of boksu, where the heuksujeo protagonist meticulously plans and executes their revenge against the geumsujeo characters who wronged them.

신분 상승 (Sinbun sangseung, shin-boon sang-seung) Upward social mobility; a rise in social status. This is the technical term for the end goal of the Spoon Class game. Every 흙수저 (heuksujeo) who studies relentlessly for an exam or works multiple jobs is dreaming of sinbun sangseung—the day they can finally break free from the limitations of their birth.

 **A Quick Pronunciation Tip for Chapter 14**

This chapter's keyword is waiting for you at every Korean front door: 신발 (sin-bal).

☑ 신 (sin): This one's tricky. It's actually closer to the English word "**sheen**." It combines a soft 'sh' sound with the long 'ee' vowel you hear in "s**ee**" or "qu**ee**n."

☑ 발 (bal): Forget the word "ball." Instead, think of the 'a' in "**spa**" or "f**a**ther." It's that open "ah" sound. Now, just add a '**b**' at the beginning and a light '**l**' sound at the end. Try saying "**bahl**."

Put them together: Shin-bal. Now you know what to take off!

The "Shoes Off" Rule

(신발 벗고 들어오세요)

There's an unwritten law in the K-drama universe that is more powerful than gravity, more consistent than the last-minute airport chase scene. It is the sacred, non-negotiable rule of taking off your shoes before entering a home.

You'll see a character running from gangsters, another rushing to a medical emergency, or one returning home after a 16-hour workday. No matter the urgency, they all pause at the entrance to do one thing: slip off their shoes.

To a viewer from a culture where wearing shoes indoors is common, this might seem like a curious, time-consuming quirk. But this isn't just about keeping the floors clean (though that's part of it). It's a deep-seated cultural code that separates the outside world from the inner sanctuary of the home.

The historical secret behind this is a uniquely Korean invention: 온돌 (ondol), the underfloor heating system. For centuries, Koreans have lived their lives on the floor—eating, socializing, studying, and sleeping on warm, heated floors. The floor isn't just for walking; it's a giant, communal piece of furniture. You wouldn't wear your dirty street shoes on your bed or your dining table, right? Same logic.

Taking off your shoes is a symbolic act. It's a sign of respect for the private, clean, and warm space of the home. It's you shedding the dirt and chaos of the outside world before stepping into a personal sanctuary.

This rule is so absolute, it becomes a powerful storytelling tool.

The Oscar-winning film [기생충, **Parasite; 2019, Hulu/Max**] uses this perfectly. The way the impoverished Kim family meticulously and automatically removes their shoes before entering the wealthy Park family's pristine home underscores how deeply this etiquette is ingrained in everyone, regardless of class. It's a basic sign of respect they must perform to maintain their cover.

You'll also notice the next level of this code in many dramas: the offering of guest slippers. In the cozy drama [갯마을 차차차, **Hometown Cha-Cha-Cha; 2021, Netflix],** the city-girl dentist Yoon Hye-jin is initially surprised by the intimate, shoes-off nature of the seaside village homes. As she begins to open her heart to the community, the simple act of a village grandmother offering her a pair of guest slippers becomes a powerful symbol. It's a sign that she is no longer an outsider, but is being welcomed into their family-like circle.

So, the threshold of a Korean home is more than just an entrance. It's a symbolic border. And the simple act of taking off your shoes is your passport to cross it, a small gesture that shows a massive amount of cultural respect.

But even with respect in your heart, navigating the details can be tricky. You probably have questions—"Wait, what if my socks have holes?!" We've got answers. Let's add the real-world plays to your social survival kit.

The **DECODER'S** Playbook

You understand why taking off shoes is so important. Here are the three most frequently asked questions from real-life visitors to Korea, answered.

Play #1: The "Is This a Shoes-Off Zone?" Play

The Pro-Tip: So, do you have to take your shoes off everywhere? No, but the list is long. Homes are a 100% shoes-off zone. Many traditional restaurants where you sit on the floor, as well as temples, also require it. Modern offices and most cafes are usually shoes-on. The golden rule? When in doubt, look down. If you see a shoe rack or a pile of shoes at the entrance, that's your cue.

Play #2: The "Awkward Sock Situation" Play

The Pro-Tip: Let's be real: this is the number one source of anxiety for many foreigners. The fear of the surprise hole in your sock is universal. Because taking off shoes is a daily event in Korea, people do tend to pay more attention to wearing nice, clean socks. So, it's a good idea to wear a decent pair if you know you'll be visiting a home. But if you get caught with a hole? Don't panic. Your host will be far too polite to ever point it out. Just curl your toes with quiet confidence and move on.

Play #3: The "Slipper Swap" Play

The Pro-Tip: You've taken off your shoes, and your host offers you guest slippers (실내화, sil-lae-hwa). Should you wear them? Yes! It's polite to accept their hospitality. But here's the advanced move: be aware of the other slippers. There will be a separate pair of plastic slippers waiting right in front of the bathroom door. These are only for the bathroom. Never, ever wear the bathroom slippers out into the main living area. Mastering the slipper swap is a true sign of a K-culture pro.

⬆ Level-Up Vocabulary

현관 (Hyeon-gwan, hyun-gwan) The entrance; the foyer. This is the official boundary line between the "outside" world and the "inside" world of the home. The hyeon-gwan is the designated area where shoes are taken off and left before stepping up into the main living space. It's the gate to the sanctuary.

실내화 (Sil-lae-hwa, shil-lae-hwa) Indoor slippers. What a thoughtful host offers you after you've taken off your shoes. Sil-lae-hwa are not for outdoor use and are a symbol of hospitality and comfort, ensuring your feet stay warm and clean inside the home. K-drama couples often have cute, matching "couple slippers."

온돌 (Ondol, ohn-dohl) The traditional Korean underfloor heating system. This is the historical "why" behind the entire shoes-off culture. Because Koreans have lived on heated floors for centuries—sitting, eating, and sleeping on them—the floor itself is treated with the same level of cleanliness as a bed or a sofa. Ondol is the reason the floor is a sacred, shoes-off space.

예의 (**Ye-ui, yeh-wee**) Manners; etiquette; courtesy. Taking off your shoes before entering someone's home is considered the most basic and fundamental ye-ui in Korea. Forgetting to do so would be a major faux pas, signaling a lack of respect for the host and their home.

들어가다 (**Deureogada, deu-ruh-ga-da**) To enter; to go in. This is the action you take only after removing your shoes at the 현관 (hyeon-gwan). When a character arrives at a door, they'll often announce their arrival by saying, "들어갑니다! (Deureogamnida!)"—"I'm coming in!"—just before they open the door and begin the shoe-removing ritual.

 **A Quick Pronunciation Tip for Chapter 15**

Let's learn the names for our two symbolic homes: 옥탑방 (ok-tap-bang) and 재벌집 (jae-beol-jip).

☑ 옥 (ok): Say "oak" like the tree, but stop the sound abruptly.

☑ 탑 (tap): Sounds exactly like the English word "top."

☑ 방 (bang): Think of the English word for a farm building: "barn." The "ba-" part is a perfect match. The only tiny difference is the ending. Instead of the 'n' sound, you need the 'ng' sound you hear in "strong" or "king." So, imagine saying "barn" but replace the final 'n' with an 'ng' sound: **Bar-n → Bah-ng → 방 (bang)**.

☑ 재 (jae): Sounds like the 'Je' in "**Je**lly."

☑ 벌 (beol): The eo sound (like 'u' in "sun") followed by a light 'l'. Try saying "buhl."

☑ 집 (jip): Sounds like the vehicle brand name, "**Jeep**."

Put them together: **Ok-tap-bang** (Rooftop room) and **Jae-beol-jip** (Chaebol house).

Rooftop Romance vs. Chaebol Palace

(옥탑방 vs. 재벌집)

In the world of K-dramas, you don't need a character's résumé to know their entire life story. You just need their address. A character's living space isn't just a background set; it's a powerful symbol of their social class, their personality, and often, their romantic destiny.

This is most obvious in the ultimate K-drama dichotomy: the humble **옥탑방 (oktapbang)**, or rooftop apartment, versus the cold, imposing **재벌집 (jaebeoljip)**, or chaebol family mansion.

The Rooftop Apartment: A Palace for Dreamers The **oktapbang** is the undisputed home of the hardworking 흙수저 (heuksujeo). In reality, it's often a more affordable housing option, but in K-dramaland, it's transformed into a romantic sanctuary. It symbolizes independence, struggle, and the freedom to dream. The classic oktapbang scene is iconic: a panoramic view of the glittering Seoul skyline at night, laundry drying on a line, and cheap plastic chairs on a green astroturf floor. This is where our hero or heroine eats instant noodles, drinks soju with their best friend, and falls in love under the stars. It's a space of authentic, heartfelt connection.

The Chaebol Mansion: The Gilded Cage On the other end of the spectrum is the jaebeoljip, the home of the 금수저 (geumsujeo). This isn't a home; it's a palace, a fortress, and most often, a gilded cage. These mansions are visually stunning but emotionally sterile. Think vast, minimalist living rooms where no one actually lives, dining tables so long that family members feel miles apart, and an atmosphere so heavy with tension you could cut it with a diamond-encrusted knife. This is a space of conflict, loneliness, and transactional relationships, where love is often the last thing on the agenda.

The contrast between these two worlds is a classic K-drama setup.

In **[쌈 마이웨이, Fight for My Way; 2017, Viki/Netflix]**, the oktapbang is the star. Think of the iconic scenes where the main characters sit on their shared rooftop space at night, surrounded by cheap plastic furniture, sharing a beer while looking at the city lights. It's in that humble, open space—not a fancy bar—that they share their deepest fears and dreams.

Conversely, the jaebeoljip is a stage for conflict. Think of the terrifyingly silent family dinner in [킹더랜드, **King the Land; 2023, Netflix**], where the main character, Gu Won, sits at an absurdly long table, separated from his family by miles of polished mahogany and unspoken resentment. The luxurious food is tasteless in the face of such emotional coldness.

The quintessential fantasy, seen in classics like [시크릿 가든, **Secret Garden; 2010, Viki/Netflix**], is when a character from the rooftop world enters the palace, or vice versa. The clash of these two symbolic spaces— the warm, authentic rooftop versus the cold, lonely mansion—is what creates the sparks, the conflict, and the unforgettable romance that we all love.

But beyond the romance, these locations are loaded with secret codes and real-life questions from fans around the world. It's time to add the final, most revealing plays to your decoder's playbook.

The **DECODER'S** Playbook

You understand the basic symbolism. But fans who fall down an internet rabbit hole often ask more specific questions. Here are the answers.

Play #1: The "Rooftop as a Magical Safe Space" Play

The Fan's Question: "Why do all the most important, heartfelt moments happen on a random rooftop? The first kiss, the deepest conversations... it always happens there!"

The Pro-Tip: You're right, it's not a coincidence. The 옥탑방 (oktapbang) in K-dramas is more than just a home; it's a "third space," a sanctuary away from the judgment of family and the pressures of society. It's physically elevated above the city, giving characters a sense of freedom and perspective. It's a liminal space where their true, unguarded feelings can finally come out. So when a confession happens on a rooftop, it's a signal that it is 100% authentic.

Play #2: The "Why Are Chaebol Houses So... Empty?" Play

The Fan's Question: "Do rich people in Korea really live in these giant, cold, museum-like houses with almost no personal items? It looks so unrealistic!"

The Pro-Tip: This is less about realism and more about symbolism. The production designer intentionally makes the 재벌집 (jaebeoljip) look vast, sterile, and empty to visually represent the family's emotional state. The cavernous living room, the ridiculously long dining table, the lack of family photos—it all screams emotional emptiness, loneliness (외로움, oeroum), and a lack of real connection (정, Jeong). The house is a beautiful prison, not a warm home.

Play #3: The "Crossing the Threshold" Play

The Fan's Question: "What's the big deal when the rich guy visits the poor girl's tiny apartment and seems amazed by her instant ramyun?"

The Pro-Tip: This is the ultimate symbolic act of the romance. When a 금수저 (geumsujeo) character willingly leaves their sterile palace to eat instant ramyun on the floor of a humble **oktapbang**, it signifies them choosing authenticity and warmth over their family's wealth. It's the moment they prove their feelings are genuine by slumming it, K-drama style. It's not just a visit; it's a declaration of which world they truly want to belong to.

Level-Up Vocabulary

보증금 (Bojeung-geum, bo-jeung-geum) / 월세 (Wolse, wol-seh) Security deposit / Monthly rent. These are the real-world terms that haunt every 흙수저 (heuksu-jeo) character. In dramas, you'll often see characters sighing over how to scrape together the bojeung-geum for a new place or worrying about being late with their wolse. These words represent the financial reality behind the romanticism of a rooftop apartment.

집사 (Jipsa, jip-sa) A butler. The quintessential resident of a 재벌집 (jaebeoljip), besides the family itself. The jipsa is often a loyal, secretive figure who knows all the family's dark secrets. The presence of a jipsa in a home is the ultimate signifier of "old money" chaebol status.

상속자 (Sangsokja, sang-sok-ja) An heir/heiress. The person who is destined to inherit the jaebeoljip and the family company. The sangsokja is the character who seemingly has everything but is often the loneliest, trapped by their family's expectations. Their story arc is usually about finding true happiness by escaping the "gilded cage."

외로움 (Oeroum, weh-roh-oom) Loneliness. This is the secret inhabitant of every grand jaebeoljip. Despite being filled with expensive art and luxurious furniture, these mansions are often portrayed as vast, empty spaces where characters feel deep oeroum. It's the emotional price they pay for their 금수저 (geumsujeo) status.

자유 (Jayu, ja-yoo) Freedom. This is the core emotional value that the 옥탑방 (oktapbang) represents. While it may be small and humble, it's a space free from the oppressive rules and expectations of a chaebol family. It's a place where characters can be their true, authentic selves, which is why so many K-drama romances blossom on rooftops.

 **A Quick Pronunciation Tip for Chapter 16**

This chapter's keyword is your ticket to glowing skin: 마스크팩 (**ma-seu-keu-paek**).

☑ 마 (**ma**): Sounds like the "ma" in "ma and pa."

☑ 스 (**seu**): This uses the tricky 으 (**eu**) vowel. Say the English word "**moon**" and notice your round lips. Now, make that same "oo" sound *without rounding your lips*. Spread your lips wide, like a flat smile, and push the sound from your throat. Add an '**s**' in front, and you get **seu**.

☑ 크 (**keu**): Same logic! It's the same 으 (eu) vowel with a '**k**' in front.

☑ 팩 (**paek**): Sounds exactly like the English word "**pack**."

Decoding the Glow: The Sheet Mask Ritual

(K-광채의 비밀: 마스크팩 의식)

The long day is over. The drama's heroine slumps onto her bed, a picture of pure exhaustion. In the next scene, she has transformed into a serene, glowing figure with a placid white sheet on her face. No, you haven't switched to a horror movie. You've just witnessed a sacred K-beauty ritual and met the K-drama world's favorite self-care tool: the 마스크팩 (maseukeupaek).

This isn't just a random spa moment; it's a cultural phenomenon and a window into the Korean obsession with 피부 관리 (pibu gwalli), or skincare. The act of putting on a sheet mask is a form of daily self-care (셀프케어, selpeuke-eo), a quiet meditation that signifies the end of the workday and the beginning of personal time.

In K-dramas, this ritual is a powerful storytelling device. It often shows a character at their most vulnerable— stripped of their makeup and their "public face." This cultural code was perfectly showcased in Episode

4 of the global hit [사랑의 불시착, **Crash Landing on You; 2019, Netflix]**. When cosmetics CEO Yoon Se-ri rewards a K-drama-loving North Korean soldier, she doesn't give him money; she gives him a sheet mask. His initial terror at the "ghostly" sheet, followed by his glowing satisfaction, is a hilarious and touching moment that bridges their two worlds. If you haven't seen it, this scene alone is worth looking up; it's guaranteed to make you laugh. Dramas focused on appearance, like [여신강림, **True Beauty; 2020, Viki]**, naturally feature sheet masks as a daily staple. And in Episode 5 of [빈센조, **Vincenzo; 2021, Netflix]**, even the tough-as-nails mafia consigliere, Vincenzo Cassano, is seen calmly using a sheet mask in his pajamas—a witty scene that proves this self-care ritual is truly for everyone.

Now that you've decoded the on-screen meaning of the sheet mask ritual, you might be tempted to try it yourself. But to get the full K-drama glow, there are a few pro-tips you need to know. Let's add them to your K-beauty playbook.

The **DECODER'S** Playbook

You know why the sheet mask appears so often. But what is it telling you as a viewer? Here are the three key plays to decode the meaning behind the mask.

Play #1: The "Vulnerability Indicator" Play

The Pro-Tip: When a character puts on a sheet mask, they are literally and figuratively putting their guard down. Pay attention to the monologue or quiet decision that happens in this scene. It's often a rare moment of the character's true, unfiltered honesty with themselves.

Play #2: The "Relationship Thermometer" Play

The Pro-Tip: The number of people in the mask scene is a huge clue about the state of a relationship. One person signifies lonely self-care. Two friends signify deep comfort. And a couple doing masks together? That's the peak of domestic bliss, a sign the Sseom phase is long over.

Play #3: The "Comedic Relief" Play

The Pro-Tip: The sheet mask is a fantastic tool for easy comedy. The classic scenario? A character is relaxing with a mask on when someone (often their love interest) unexpectedly visits. The resulting "ghost!" scream or the awkward conversation is a beloved trope used to break tension and create a funny, memorable moment.

Level-Up Vocabulary

피부 (Pibu, pee-boo) Skin. The canvas for all of K-beauty. In dramas, having good `pibu` is often seen as a sign of good health and self-care.

피부 관리 (Pibu gwalli, pee-boo gwan-lee) Skincare. This is the entire philosophy and industry. It's not just about makeup; it's about a consistent routine to achieve healthy skin from the inside out.

셀프케어 (Selpeuke-eo, sel-puh-keh-uh) Self-care. A Konglish term that has become a huge part of modern Korean culture. The sheet mask ritual is the ultimate form of `selpeuke-eo`—a small, affordable luxury to de-stress and take care of yourself.

보습 (Boseup, bo-seup) Moisturizing; hydration. This is the number one goal of most Korean skincare routines and the primary function of most sheet masks. Achieving moist, dewy, "chok-chok" skin is the holy grail.

꿀피부 (**Kkul-pibu, kkool-pee-boo**) Honey skin. The highest compliment. This doesn't mean your skin is sticky; it means it's so healthy, hydrated, and glowing that it looks as smooth and luminous as honey. This is the goal of every sheet mask session.

The Post-Credits Scene

And just like that, the final credits are rolling... on this book.

We started this journey with a simple feeling—that when we watch K-dramas, there's always something more just beneath the surface. Together, we've traveled through the three great codes of the K-drama universe. We decoded the hidden meanings in their words (The Verbal Code), unlocked the unspoken rules of their relationships (The Social Code), and revealed the beautiful traditions that shape their daily lives (The Life Code).

The biggest secret we've decoded, however, isn't a single word or a cultural rule. It's a new way of seeing. It's the realization that every K-drama is a rich, complex world layered with history, emotion, and nuance that subtitles can never fully capture. You now have the tools to see it all. You are no longer just a fan watching from the outside; you are an insider who understands the "why" behind the "what."

So, what happens now?

Your next K-drama marathon is about to feel completely different. Every shared soju glass will be a story of respect. Every bowl of birthday soup will be a tribute to a mother's love. Every awkward silence and every casual Hwaiting! will have a new, deeper layer of meaning. The shows haven't changed, but your eyes have.

The final credits on this book may be rolling, but your new K-drama journey is just beginning.

Enjoy the show!

A Final Word & Thank You

Thank you for reading!

If you enjoyed decoding K-dramas with us, please consider leaving an honest review on Amazon. Your review is the best way to help fellow fans discover this book.

You can go directly to the review page by using the link below or scanning the QR code.

Linktr.ee/JunghoPark

A portion of the profit from sales of this book will be donated to:

1. American Civil Liberties Union (www.aclu.org)
2. Habitat for Humanity Korea (www.habitat.or.kr)

Pronunciation Appendix

Welcome to your pronunciation command center! You've learned the codes, the plays, and the vocabulary. This appendix is your final tool to make sure that when you speak these words, you sound as confident as you feel.

Think of this as your personal reference guide. The first part covers the key rules of Korean pronunciation, and the second part is a dictionary of all the fun terms we learned together.

Part 1: The Golden Rules of Pronunciation

1. The Vowel Code: It's All in the Lip Shape

- ㅏ (a) vs. ㅓ (eo): The 'a' in 반찬 (banchan) is the open "**ah**" sound. The 'eo' in 언니 (eonni) is the relaxed "**uh**" sound, like in "s**u**n."

- ㅗ (o) vs. ㅜ (u): The 'o' in 오빠 (oppa) is made with round lips, like the "o" in "go." The 'u' in 우리 (uri) is also made with round lips, but sounds like the "oo" in "m**oo**n."

- **The Trickiest Vowel**: ㅡ (eu): The secret to 금 (geum) is to make the "oo" sound from "m**oo**n" *without rounding your lips*. Spread your lips wide like a flat smile and make the sound from your throat.

2. The Consonant Code: The Three Brothers

Many Korean consonants come in a set of three: a normal sound, a strong (airy) sound, and a sharp (tense) sound. It's all about the air!

The Three Brothers	Vibe Check	How it Feels (Air & Pitch)
Normal: ㅂ (b/p)	Soft 'b' sound.	Mid-pitch, relaxed.
STRONG: ㅍ (p)	Breathy 'p' sound.	High-pitch, **lots of air!**
SHARP: ㅃ (pp)	Sharp, hard 'b' sound.	High-pitch, N**O AIR!**

Normal: ㄷ (d/t)	Soft 'd' sound.	Mid-pitch, relaxed.

The Three Brothers	Vibe Check	How it Feels (Air & Pitch)
STRONG: ㅌ (t)	Breathy 't' sound.	High-pitch, **lots of air!**
SHARP: ㄸ (tt)	Sharp, hard 'd' sound.	High-pitch, **NO AIR!**

Normal: ㅅ (s)	Soft 's' sound.	Mid-pitch, relaxed.
SHARP: ㅆ (ss)	Sharp, hissy 's' sound.	High-pitch, **NO AIR!**

Part 2: The K-Drama Decoder's Dictionary

- 2차 (**I-cha**): Second round (of a night out).
- 애정 표현 (**Aejeong pyohyeon**): An expression of affection.
- 애매하다 (**Aemaehada**): To be vague, ambiguous.
- 어색하다 (**Eosaekhada**): To be awkward.
- 어장관리 (**Eojang-gwanli**): "Fish farm management"; stringing multiple people along.
- 어머니 (**Eomeoni**): Mother (formal).
- 언니 (**Eonni**): What a female calls an older sister or close female friend.
- 배달 (**Baedal**): Delivery.
- 반찬 (**Banchan**): Side dishes.

- **반말 (Banmal)**: Casual, informal speech.
- **발 (Bal)**: Foot.
- **밥 (Bap)**: Cooked rice; a meal.
- **방 (Bang)**: Room.
- **보습 (Boseup)**: Moisturizing; hydration.
- **보증금 (Bojeung-geum)**: Security deposit.
- **복수 (Boksu)**: Revenge.
- **부담스럽다 (Budamseureopda)**: To feel burdened or uncomfortable.
- **부자 (Buja)**: A rich person.
- **챙겨주다 (Chaeng-gyeo-juda)**: To take care of someone.
- **축하하다 (Chukahada)**: To congratulate; to celebrate.
- **친구 (Chingu)**: Friend.
- **다정하다 (Dajeonghada)**: To be sweet, kind, or affectionate.
- **단무지 (Danmuji)**: Yellow pickled radish.
- **대박 (Daebak)**: Awesome; a great success.
- **대표님 (Daepyonim)**: CEO; representative director.
- **동갑 (Dong-gap)**: A person who is the same age as you.
- **들어가다 (Deureogada)**: To enter; to go in.
- **응원하다 (Eungwonhada)**: To cheer for; to support.

- **가난 (Ganan)**: Poverty.
- **감사 (Gamsa)**: Gratitude; thanks.
- **개천에서 용 난다 (Gaecheon-eseo yong nanda)**: "A dragon rises from a ditch"; a rags-to-riches story.
- **거절하다 (Geojeolhada)**: To refuse; to reject.
- **건배 (Geonbae)**: Cheers!
- **걱정하다 (Geokjeonghada)**: To worry.
- **고백하다 (Gobaekhada)**: To confess (one's romantic feelings).
- **공동체 (Gongdongche)**: A community; a collective.
- **괜찮아요 (Gwaenchanayo)**: "It's okay"; "Are you okay?"; "No, thank you."
- **한턱내다 (Hanteok-naeda)**: To treat someone to a meal or drinks.
- **회식 (Hoesik)**: A company dinner.
- **후배 (Hoobae)**: A junior colleague or student.
- **후회하다 (Huhoehada)**: To regret.
- **화이팅 (Hwaiting)**: "Fighting!"; a cheer of encouragement.
- **형 (Hyeong)**: What a male calls an older brother or close male friend.
- **흙수저 (Heuk-su-jeo)**: "Dirt spoon"; someone from a poor background.
- **힘내다 (Himnaeda)**: To cheer up; to be strong.

- **인사치레 (Insachire)**: Lip service; a polite pleasantry.
- **이사 (Isa)**: Moving; moving houses.
- **자유 (Jayu)**: Freedom.
- **잘못 (Jalmot)**: A fault; a wrongdoing.
- **재벌집 (Jaebeol-jip)**: A chaebol house; a mansion.
- **정 (Jeong)**: A deep, emotional connection and affection.
- **젓가락 (Jeotgarak)**: Chopsticks.
- **집 (Jip)**: House; home.
- **집들이 (Jipdeuri)**: A housewarming party.
- **집사 (Jipsa)**: A butler.
- **존댓말 (Jondaetmal)**: Formal, polite speech.
- **주량 (Juryang)**: Drinking capacity.
- **주사 (Jusa)**: Drunken habits (often negative).
- **중국집 (Junggukjip)**: A Korean-style Chinese restaurant.
- **기운 (Gi-un)**: Energy; vigor.
- **금수저 (Geum-su-jeo)**: "Gold spoon"; someone from a rich background.
- **꿀피부 (Kkul-pibu)**: "Honey skin"; flawless, glowing skin.
- **꿈 (Kkum)**: Dream.
- **말을 놓다 (Mareul nota)**: To drop formalities; to speak Banmal.

- **말을 높이다 (Mareul nopida)**: To speak more formally.
- **마스크팩 (Maseukeupaek)**: Sheet mask.
- **맛집 (Matjip):** A famous/delicious restaurant.
- **미안해 (Mianhae)**: "I'm sorry" (casual).
- **미역국 (Miyeokguk)**: Seaweed soup.
- **밀당 (Mildang)**: Push-pull (in a relationship).
- **나이 (Nai)**: Age.
- **남 (Nam)**: An outsider; a stranger.
- **내 편 (Nae pyeon)**: My side; my person.
- **...님 (Nim)**: An honorific suffix for respect.
- **누나 (Nuna)**: What a male calls an older sister or close female friend.
- **오해 (Ohae)**: A misunderstanding.
- **옥탑방 (Oktapbang)**: A rooftop room/apartment.
- **온돌 (Ondol)**: Korean underfloor heating system.
- **오빠 (Oppa)**: What a female calls an older brother or close male friend.
- **외로움 (Oeroum)**: Loneliness.
- **피부 (Pibu)**: Skin.
- **피부 관리 (Pibu gwalli)**: Skincare.
- **편하게 (Pyeonhage)**: Comfortably; casually.
- **포기하다 (Pogihada)**: To give up.

- **사과하다 (Sagwahada)**: To apologize (formal verb).
- **사귀다 (Sagwida)**: To date; to be in a relationship.
- **상속자 (Sangsokja)**: An heir/heiress.
- **선물 (Seonmul)**: A gift; a present.
- **선배 (Seonbae)**: A senior colleague or student.
- **성공 (Seonggong)**: Success.
- **섭섭하다 (Seopseop-hada)**: To feel sad or disappointed by someone close.
- **셀프케어 (Selpeuke-eo)**: Self-care (Konglish).
- **생일 (Saeng-il)**: Birthday.
- **신발 (Sin-bal)**: Shoes.
- **신분 상승 (Sinbun sangseung)**: Upward social mobility.
- **신경쓰다 (Sin-gyeong-sseu-da)**: To care about; to be bothered by.
- **식구 (Sikgu)**: Family members; "one who shares meals."
- **실내화 (Sil-lae-hwa)**: Indoor slippers.
- **실수 (Silsu)**: A mistake; an error.
- **술버릇 (Sulbeoreut)**: Drinking habits.
- **썸 (Sseom)**: The ambiguous pre-dating stage; "something."
- **우리 (Uri)**: We; our.
- **약속 (Yaksok)**: A promise; an appointment.

- **예의 (Ye-ui)**: Manners; etiquette.
- **용서하다 (Yongseohada)**: To forgive.
- **용기 (Yong-gi)**: Courage.
- **원샷 (Wonshot)**: One-shot; bottoms up (Konglish).
- **월세 (Wolse)**: Monthly rent.
- **짠 (Jjan)**: Cheers! (casual).
- **죄송합니다 (Joesonghamnida)**: "I'm sorry" (formal).

About the Author

Jungho Park is a native Korean speaker from the beautiful harbor city of Busan in South Korea. Tutoring both Korean and English has been a big part of his life, alongside his professions in the Aviation and Corporate Finance fields.

Following the success of his #1 Bestseller and Hottest New Release, How to Speak KPOP, his "How to Speak K-" series continues with his latest book, How to Speak K-DRAMA. His dream is to create fun, witty, and accessible guides that help Korean culture enthusiasts go beyond the subtitles and truly understand the world they love.

He can usually be found dancing to K-POP in his kitchen while waiting for the next K-drama episode to load, or passionately explaining to his fur-daughter Jindo Snowy why the male lead absolutely should not have gotten on that plane to America.

Send him a fan mail: theauthorjp@gmail.com